SOUL SEARCH

SOUL SEARCH

THE HEALING POSSIBILITIES OF PAST LIVES

by Edward Klein, M.D.

ASSOCIATION FOR
RESEARCH AND
ENLIGHTENMENT

A.R.E. Press • Virginia Beach • Virginia

A.R.E. Press
Sixty-Eighth & Atlantic Avenue
P.O. Box 656
Virginia Beach, VA 23451-0656

Library of Congress Cataloging-in-Publication Data
Klein, Edward, 1940-
    Soul search : the healing possibilities of past lives / by Ed-
ward Klein.
        p.   cm.
    ISBN 0-87604-341-4
    1. Reincarnation therapy. 2. Reincarnation therapy—Case
studies. I. Title.
RC489.R43K54   1995
616.89'14—dc20   95-23277

Cover design by Richard Boyle

"Live so that thou mayest desire to live again—
that is thy duty;
for, in any case, thou wilt live again!"

—Nietzsche

Contents

Acknowledgments

How does one start? To those who have contributed, in their own different ways, my appreciation knows no limits. However, there are those special people who, without them, this project would never have been born. For a long time, the thought of a book remained just that—a thought. Not until my wife, Liz, kept reminding me—"If you want it bad enough, do it. Get off your butt"—did the thought start to germinate. Finally, I heard the message and, once begun, I couldn't have been happier, for this truly has been a labor of love. So first on my list is a heartfelt thanks to Liz.

To my daughters, Debbie and Laurie—"You see, I made it." Never a moment's doubt in their minds. These two young women have been a source of continuous encouragement. Always positive, they exhibit an enthusiasm that is contagious—even when they look at me as a somewhat different father and lovingly exclaim, "Dad, oh Dad."

To Carol, my co-author, I can't thank her enough. She plunged into our work with a commitment nonparalleled. An accomplished writer, she remained quite patient as I began the journey into what was for me, a new field—that of journalism. Her guidance throughout helped eliminate any fears I might have harbored about writing. She continued, throughout our book, to be as energetic at the end as she was at the beginning.

To my office manager, Judy, who helped with transcriptions, faxes, and general organization, a sincere thanks.

To Ken Skidmore, my editor from A.R.E., I want to acknowledge a developing relationship that is presently being solidified. Ken has helped immensely with the finalization of my working with the publishing house. I've enjoyed his input and can only look forward to cementing the ties with him and A.R.E.

Lastly, before ending these thoughts, I wish to acknowledge and thank my predecessors who, over the years, decided to veer from the conventional arena and present their works. The road has opened, and I'm pleased to be able to "step up to the plate" and join those who are willing to move forward with their beliefs, different as they may be.

INTRODUCTION

*T*he story you are about to read is true, which only shows the accuracy of the statement, "Truth is stranger than fiction." Ten years ago, I myself might have doubted such a tale. My training is that of a scientist: One must see it to believe it. But as a psychiatrist, I have learned to keep an open mind, understanding that things are not always as they seem and that there is much about the mysteries of the human mind that we do not as yet understand.

Throughout my life, I had always traveled a traditional path. This carried through to my professional life as well. After graduating from the University of Louisville Medical School in 1966, I took my psychiatric residency at the internationally known NYU Bellevue Hospital Center, where I was chief resident in 1969-'70. The only national attention I've ever received was through my work in professional sports and stress management, although I did serve as a consultant to one of the NFL teams. I've been married to the same woman for twenty-seven years and have two grown daughters.

My life was conservative and not particularly unusual. It wasn't, that is, until a few years ago when some unexplained events took place that led me to begin questioning some long-standing beliefs. The focus of my work shifted, at first ever so slightly, then dramatically.

For more than twenty years, I have used hypnosis to help specific patients access memories. By uncovering and dealing with these memories, individuals may be able to work through problems confronting them in their daily lives.

One therapeutic use of hypnosis is that of "age regression." This involves putting the person into the hypnotic state and then regressing him or her to childhood, to search for trauma, phobias, or fears that may have occurred at that vulnerable time. I've used this type of treatment successfully with some patients.

In 1982, I used age regression with a particular patient, suggesting that she would regress to age fourteen. Suddenly, however, without any prompting from me, she began to speak with a strange accent. When I asked her the year, she took my pencil and wrote, "IV."

Needless to say, I was shaken. Obviously, I was not about to announce that I thought I had regressed someone to a past life, one almost 2,000 years ago. Instead, I kept the bizarre incident to myself.

Then, gradually, a series of strange events began to occur. At the same time, I also began to investigate the study of past lives and used that as a basis for my work with specific patients. As my case histories grew, my thoughts turned toward putting my voluminous notes into book form.

But I had no experience in writing a full-length book. I instinctively knew that I would need help from a writer. From my subconscious, a name appeared. It was a medical writer I had met through my children's school. On impulse, I called her.

Soul Search is the story of what happened when "Carol," as she prefers to be known, and I began to work together. We tell our story in two voices, because we felt it best offered readers the opportunity to experience past-life regression through Carol's encounters and vivid descriptions. My comments serve as narration, to describe what is occurring from medical and scientific aspects.

Alternating voices in a conversational style, we present a story that ultimately takes the reader all over the world, throughout many different time periods and numerous lives. We share with Carol her initial reluctance amid skepticism, and the gradual acceptance of what she was seeing and feeling. We witness the resolution of various issues. Gently, I offered her guidance with objective and therapeutic interpretations.

I am not the first psychiatrist who has dealt with this unexpected turn of events, where observation defies scientific explanation. Nor will I be the last. But I remain open to explore the possibilities and invite the reader to do the same.

The late Edgar Cayce, internationally known psychic and healer, gave many "life readings," in which he stressed the unity of the body, the soul, and the Universal Force we all share. Although he died in 1945, Cayce offered numerous predictions, many of which have come true. Much has been written on telepathy, precognition, ESP, and reincarnation using his psychic readings as source material. One of Cayce's sons, the late Hugh Lynn Cayce, said, "I think we are in a new age of humanity's discoveries."

I agree.

PROLOGUE

DR. KLEIN

*F*ebruary 18, 1992, I made a phone call to a medical writer. That impulsive act was to forever alter the focus of both our lives.

CAROL

1945: I was eight years old, flying with my father over Midwestern farm lands in his two-engine Piper Cub. He banked the airplane and pointed.

"Look at those fields. It looks like a checkerboard, doesn't it?"

I turned my head in the direction he was pointing and shut my eyes. I couldn't bear to let him know the view terrified me. There was no way I could look down.

1982: My husband and I took our children on a long-awaited vacation out West through the Colorado Rockies. What had seemed like a dream trip, however, became a nightmare for me as he steered our oversized rental van around hairpin turns and along narrow roadways with treacherous cliffs and no side rails. I clung to the seat of the passenger side in front, trying to still my anxiety and keep from whimpering or crying out. It was with great relief for all when we came to the Continental Divide, where we could pull off in a picture-taking area and I could retreat to a back seat on the driver's side.

1991: My husband and I and our youngest child traveled together on a trip to Paris. While my son and husband took the elevator to the top of the Eiffel Tower, I wandered around on the ground below, angry that my irrational fear of heights had prevented my enjoying the view from the top as well.

Then . . .

1992: I climbed to the top of a thirty-foot scaffolding erected by a builder so that my husband and I could get an idea of the view from the upstairs bedroom of our proposed new home.

1992: I took the glass elevator to the top of the Marriotte Marquis on New York's Broadway and, for the first time, enjoyed the view it offered.

1992: I looked down from a plane which was about to land at New York's La Guardia airport without clutching my husband in panic.

What had changed? What erased my fear of heights?

Past-life therapy.

DR. KLEIN

If anyone had asked, I would have told that person that I've always thought of myself as a fairly conservative type—traditional with a capital "T"—especially as it relates to my medical practice. I received my medical degree from the University of Louisville Medical School in 1966. My psychiatric residency was at NYU's Bellevue Hospital Center, where I was chief resident in 1969-'70. Subsequently, I entered the military and was a lieutenant commander at a major naval teaching hospital.

Afterward, I eventually settled in Tampa, Florida, and have been practicing psychiatry there since 1973. I've received national attention through my work in professional sports and stress management. Over the years I have also served as a consultant to one of the NFL teams.

For the past twenty years I've been working with hypnosis, which I had learned during my psychiatric residency at Bellevue. My work has been varied and includes writing and producing a video for stress control, which became part of a program developed by the Florida affiliate of the American Heart Association. All in all, my life was progressing smoothly—no bumps or curves.

My mind was not closed, but a straight path had been set.

It would have remained that way had not three dissimilar experiences taken place that would eventually affect my thinking, my work, my very existence.

In 1982 I was treating a particular patient, using age regression. The process is to put the individual into a hypnotic state and then regress him or her to childhood, where many traumas, phobias, and fears originate. The trance state is the same as the alpha state when we dream. It is here that we are in the subconscious, and it is here where we can treat a number of different phobias. Often the patient actually remembers events that took place in infancy and sometimes even in the prebirth state.

I had given this patient the suggestion that she would regress to age fourteen so that we could get to the basis of some of her problems. Suddenly and spontaneously, she regressed to a past life and began to speak with a strange accent. I didn't know what was going on. I handed her the pencil I was using.

"What's this?" she quickly responded. I told her it was a writing implement and asked her to write the year. Without hesitating, she clutched the pencil and wrote, "IV."

Obviously, someone—especially a psychiatrist with a thriving practice and a respected standing in the community—doesn't go running around broadcasting that he's just regressed a patient to a past life in the year 4 A.D.

For years, I kept this bizarre experience to myself, not daring to share it with my peers. My work with past-life therapy proceeded very slowly until two strange happenings occurred.

About three years ago, every time I started my car I'd hear screeching brakes and the sound of a crash. No one else could hear it, but I couldn't get the sound out of my head. Needless to say, it began to concern me.

Then, one night, my wife and I were coming home after dark. As we were waiting at a light, a car turned into us. The brakes screeched, metal met metal, and we were thrown to the back, still buckled into the damaged front seats.

My next recollection was vague, but somewhere I heard my wife saying—"Let's get out of here." Slowly my mind focused; I knew what I wanted to do, but much to my horror I couldn't. My brain said "move," but my body wouldn't react. Fear took over. Visions of the future were overwhelming. It seemed as if an eternity had passed and I was in a time warp. Quadriplegia.

Fortunately, the paralysis lasted only about a minute or so. Slowly, a tingling began in my feet and then in my hands. Gradually, muscle control returned. By the time the ambulance reached the hospital much of my functioning was normal. I remained in the hospital a couple of days alternating between thanking my lucky stars and reliving the terror of what had almost occurred.

I knew that somehow I had changed. Later, it also

dawned on me that the crash sound I had heard every time I entered my car was gone.

This phenomenon is called "precognition." Although there are many reports of similar strange, unexplained feelings that predict events that actually do follow—and I have had patients who claimed similar stories—this was the first time I had experienced it.

Several months later, the second unexplained experience took place.

I went to our property manager's office without telling anyone where I was going. While there, the phone rang and the receptionist handed me the receiver saying, "It's for you."

I don't recall the conversation, but afterward I realized that no one knew of my whereabouts. The caller never identified himself, but had asked for me by name. Being curious, I quickly checked the phone number there to see if it had any similarity to my office number. It didn't; not even close. I sat there, perplexed. How could someone have made this call knowing I would be here? Why would he have called me here? It was strange.

By chance, I had earlier stumbled across past-life therapy. Now, something had changed. A pattern was forming. Slowly I began to realize that what had begun with the past-life experience, then with my accident, and finally with this phone call were all related. The unknown was being presented. My thoughts were being stimulated. Would I fall back to the acceptable and well established—or would I take a chance? Was I willing to look beyond solid scientific proof?

With time and great deliberation, I decided to accept the challenge. I would begin the search. The straight path would be expanded with acknowledged new trails and bumps. I would explore. The risks that might follow were acceptable. I might incur the inevitable questions as well as possible jokes from some of my colleagues. But I knew I could help,

help resolve troubling issues that my patients were presented with. The decision was solidified. I would continue my investigation into the healing possibilities of past lives.

1

NOTHING IN LIFE IS A COINCIDENCE

DR. KLEIN

*F*reud said that nothing in life is a coincidence. All of us bear witness to its accuracy. You accept a blind date to a party you really don't want to go to and meet your future significant other who also had a blind date and didn't want to attend. You miss a plane flight and end up on a roundabout route, where you sit next to someone who gives you an important business opportunity. You stop by the neighborhood soda fountain for some ice cream and are discovered by a Hollywood producer who makes you into a famous movie star. All coincidences?

The way this book was born is one more of life's "coincidences."

I had considered writing a book about my work with past-life therapy, but found it difficult to make myself sit and begin. The ideas flowed—but as quickly as they came, they just as quickly left, without anything ever having been committed to paper. My schedule was full.

I found myself offering one excuse after another as to why I wasn't writing. Soon, however, it became evident that my work was important enough that it needed to be shared so that others could benefit.

Finally, my wife gave me the needed push. "Get off your butt and do it. Rearrange your schedule. If you want it badly enough, you can make it happen."

Thus, I mobilized myself. Instead of excuses, I looked for ways to establish a plan. How would the material be presented? What would be the best method? It soon became obvious that I needed a co-author. As I had never written a book before, I thought it best to work with an accomplished author—one who had experience in the medical field.

But how would I find such a person? It was then that I recalled meeting Carol (not her real name)—the mother of one of my daughter's friends. We had met several times due to our children's activities. I assume that I must have heard about her writings as she was fairly well known in our area, but I had never read any of her books or articles. Although we had only spoken casually in the past, she must have made an impression, because years later, when I needed a writer, I remembered her.

CAROL

On February 18, 1992, I was on a deadline to complete the manuscript for my latest book. I had been working on this particular project for the past year and a half. It had been on a complicated medical subject written for a general lay readership and had required extensive research and rewrites. I was exhausted. I looked forward to a few months of mindless relaxation and catching up on everything that is left undone when deadline looms. I had told my secretary that I was not taking any calls, was not to be disturbed unless it was an emergency. Nevertheless, she buzzed me with a call.

"A Dr. Edward Klein is on the phone," she said. "Do you want to talk to him?"

I had to stop and think for a minute before placing the name. I knew he was a local psychiatrist, although I thought of him more as the father of my child's classmate. I had spoken with him at a few of our kids' birthday parties about ten years ago, but not in any depth. I had never interviewed him for any of my medically oriented articles or books. I wasn't even sure that I remembered what he looked like.

Although I still don't know why, I agreed to take the call and pushed aside my manuscript.

After a few pleasantries he asked, "Are you interested in talking about regression?"

"What kind of regression?"

"Into past lives."

My heart skipped a beat. I paused for only a moment, then jumped across the chasm that would take me into a new world that challenged old beliefs. "Yes," I answered.

I was a believer—in concept. It's easy to be a believer. Age regression, that is, taking patients back into their childhoods in order to learn the basis for problems in adulthood, has long been an accepted form of psychotherapy. But beyond that? Into past lives? Yes. I believed in past lives, in theory. I had read a few books on the subject and listened to others tell their strange tales.

Like you, no doubt, I also have had the occasional odd experience, the "haven't I been here before?" or the "I knew what he was going to say before he said it" feeling.

Once, while driving home, I suddenly was overwhelmed by the scent of my mother-in-law's favorite cologne—"Blue Grass"—coming from the back of my car. I turned around to look, but, of course, my mother-in-law wasn't there. She had died ten years earlier.

There were other stories whispered hesitantly by acquaintances who worried that they might not be taken seriously. A friend of Irish descent visited centuries-old castles when she was in Ireland. While in one of them, however, she suddenly developed an anxiety attack and raced from the castle, unable to shake off her feeling of dread. Later, reading about the castle, she learned that an entire family with her maiden surname had been wiped out by neighboring tribes hundreds of years ago.

Another acquaintance related a dream in which he had lived in Paris during the eighteenth century. While recently visiting that city on a holiday, he not only found the street he had seen in his dream, but also recognized the home that had belonged to his family in the dream.

I consider myself to be a serious medical writer. I was just completing a nonfiction book written with a world-renowned physician. My work is carefully researched and documented. I've also been published on a myriad of medical topics. My books have been well accepted in both the medical and lay communities, receiving awards for their effectiveness, and have been translated into other languages. Serious stuff. Now . . . reincarnation? Past-life therapy?

"Well," said the doctor. "How should we do this?"

I didn't miss a beat. The fatigue factor was gone. "Set a date now," I answered. "As soon as I finish this manuscript, we'll get together for an interview." Then I laughed. "We'll see what our karma has in mind for us."

DR. KLEIN

Coincidence that we had met in the past? We don't believe so. Coincidental that our children were schoolmates and friends? We don't believe so. The stage had been set and the story was now to be told.

2

The First Meeting

CAROL

My first meeting with Dr. Klein was March 25, 1992. Uncertain of how long it would take me to get to his office on the other side of town, I arrived early. I gave my name to his secretary and had time to look around his outer office.

The reception area was typical of those found in most physicians' offices: a stack of aging *People* and *Time* magazines, a nondescript overstuffed couch, and a few chairs. In one corner, an aquarium bubbled, giving those waiting something sprightly to observe.

The door to the inner offices opened and a man entered. "Hi, I'm Ed Klein. It's good to see you again." He was of aver-

age build, trim, with an easy smile. I think I would have recognized him again even if he hadn't identified himself. His
handshake was firm, yet gentle. He motioned me to go
down the hall and into his office.

Had I thought about it or been given to preconceived
ideas, I might have expected the personal office of someone dealing with past-life regression to be flamboyant or, at
the least, ultramodern. Dr. Klein's was anything but. It was
cozy . . . safe. There was a small wooden desk with a twelve-
inch aquarium housing two tiny guppies in one corner, a
traditional couch covered in brown fabric along the far side
wall, and two well-used swivel easy chairs facing one another on the other side. Behind the chair he waved for me
to take was a small table with a clock, so he could take sur-
reptitious glances at it in order to know when to conclude a
therapeutic session with his patient.

After a little small talk and comparing what our young-
sters were presently doing, I took out my reporter's notebook. "Well," I said, "tell me about the work you're doing
with past-life regressions. It sounds fascinating."

Very shortly I was to learn just how fascinating it could
be.

DR. KLEIN

When Carol came for our first meeting, I wasn't quite sure
what to expect. My thoughts didn't revolve around her
personally, but rather focused on her receptivity—or
nonreceptivity—to my work. Would she dismiss past-life
therapy as "too weird" or would she find it interesting and
want to know more? If the latter, would she be caught up in
the idea enough that she would be willing to co-author the
book with me? If so, what would be *her* conception of the
book?

With my patients, the first couple of sessions are usually
straightforward. I take a detailed history. Then I devise a

treatment plan and discuss it with the patient. If I determine that hypnosis and past-life therapy is warranted, I'll describe the entire process to minimize fear or apprehension before we begin. I encourage questions.

It is only after all of the above occurs that I begin with the first hypnotic session. Afterward, I'll discuss the experience with the patient. If all is positive, it is only then that we'll begin work with therapy utilizing the method of past lives.

But this interview with Carol was different. She was a reporter—a professional medical writer, not a patient. I wasn't sure how we should proceed and shared my feelings with her.

CAROL

"That's no problem," I told him. I was quite comfortable with the interview situation, having interviewed many of the top medical specialists in America. "Let's begin by my asking all the questions I have and your giving me the answers. Start with your explaining just what past-life therapy is."

I could tell that now he was comfortable with our direction. We were on safe turf, discussing familiar material, something that he had been living with for ten years.

He leaned back in his chair and began. "Past-life therapy is primarily a way of accessing the subconscious mind. The patients with whom I work have many different problems. Areas of concern are varied, and roots often are deep and intertwined," he said as he obviously had done many times before.

"We are all complex, and each of us has a unique past. By the very nature of our complexities, therapy can often be drawn out over a long period. Time-honored psychotherapy is a process that can be slow. However, by the use of hypnosis and past-life therapy, the subconscious mind readily yields information. This is truly a faster way to resolve many issues that we face."

His enthusiasm was obvious as he warmed to his topic. "We resolve the issues of today by experiencing and understanding the problems as they arose in a past life. By realizing the etiology of the dynamics, acknowledging the lessons learned, and making these lessons applicable to the present life, resolutions of problems are often achieved."

"Aren't you talking about reincarnation?" I asked.

"Well, many proponents of past-life therapy advocate it as a definitive proof of reincarnation, but you don't have to believe in reincarnation for the treatment to be effective."

"Obviously this is not a unique concept," I said. "Have you done much reading on the subject? And if so, whose work?"

"I found my recollections of the Edgar Cayce material to be most helpful," he answered, leaning forward. "I had read a number of books about him years ago, but it wasn't until my own interests evolved that I understood how completely his concepts expressed my personal thoughts. It was and is like a 'gloved' fit."

"In what way?" I, too, had read some of Cayce's work, although it had been close to twenty years ago. I searched my memory in vain to recall specifics. For some unknown reason, I seemed to have blocked them out.

"Cayce, in his philosophy, helped me to work out the development of my own 'level of comfort' with reincarnation. I struggled, as one trained in the hard sciences would, with the how and why. I demanded proof as I had been trained to do. For a long while, I just could not accept what was right before me.

"Hugh Lynn Cayce wrote of his father, Edgar Cayce, 'Each soul [which Cayce sometimes called an "entity"], as it re-enters the Earth plane [or dimension] as a human being, has subconscious access to the characteristic mental capacities and skills it has accumulated in previous lives.'[1]

"Now I could understand: for it is my belief that the subconscious is part of our soul and thus travels with the soul from one body to the next, taking with it all the knowledge gained in each lifetime. This is the constant. The variable is the body the soul may enter in whatever time period selected. Therefore, when we hypnotize, we are accessing the subconscious and touching the memories. When we travel to another lifetime, the subconscious, which has stored everything, now can reveal knowledge from the previous life."

"All of our subconscious memories remain with us?" I asked. "Forever?"

"Forever, from one life to the next," Dr. Klein said. "According to Cayce, the subconscious mind has survived because 'it neither consists of, nor depends on, matter. It now becomes the conscious mind of the soul, and will continue to function as such until the soul returns into the Earth's dense matter to begin its next life.'[2] That's a direct quote," he added leaning back in his chair.

"Why do you think we are here now in this particular body?" I was finding this conversation to be a stimulating one, raising questions I had not considered before. "Are we supposed to behave in a specified manner?"

"I don't think so," he replied. "I believe that we are influenced by our karma, but still have the power of free will; our destiny or future is not predetermined. This is also supported by Cayce, who said, 'While personal destiny awaiting a given soul may consist of the inevitable consequences of his own past actions (and thus lend itself psychic predetermination) the future can never be entirely preordained.' "[3]

I pondered what he had said. "From where then did or does the soul come?" I asked at last.

"I believe that it was or is created by God and continues to be part of Him. With free will, we can go back to our Creator or we can stray. Therefore, when we are able to resolve our karma, the next step has been achieved, allowing entry to the next level, for our return to God. Cayce also noted, 'Now, He can only wait in patience and genuine compassion for the souls to decide how soon they will use their free will to return to Him, once they have concluded that He makes a better creator than they do.' "[4]

I grew thoughtful for a moment. "What if these 'past lives' are just in the person's imagination . . . if he or she is just having a good fantasy?"

"It still doesn't matter," he said, leaning forward intently again. "The important thing is that by using past-life therapy, we—and I say 'we' because other qualified therapists are using this form of treatment successfully as well—we are making people better. And that's our job, to make people feel better and cope more effectively."

I nodded. "Do you use past-life therapy in much of your practice?"

"I'd say with about thirty to forty percent of my patients now, when it's warranted."

"And it's proven effective?"

"I've recorded success with a number of those suffering from anxiety attacks, stress, weight problems, sexual dysfunction, fears, phobias, or psychosomatic illness."

I looked down at my notes. "How many past lives do you think a person has?"

"It's hard to answer," he said. "Although I do believe that there are many over the ages. We have the option to come back when we want to resolve the issues that haven't been worked out."

"Here's another question," I said. "As you mentioned earlier, the idea that past-life problems may cause difficulties in our present life isn't a new one, but why, now of all times, has there been a resurgence of interest in past lives?"

"That's what makes all this so exciting," he said. "Many more people are now searching for and opening themselves to new ideas, new possibilities. We, as a society, are not as rigid as we used to be. In fact, many professionals are now responding by writing and lecturing in public about what used to be discussed only in hallways."

I looked up from my notebook, paused, and stared him

directly in the eye. "Do *you* believe that your patients access their past lives?"

"I do," he said without hesitation. "I've seen their reactions here in this very room. They *are* experiencing. Past-life therapy offers them a safe form of therapeutic intervention. It allows a patient to examine traumatic or troubling experiences in a nonthreatening environment, sometimes being effective after just one session."

"Why don't more therapists use this modality?" I asked.

"Many of them have trouble accepting the concept of past lives," he explained simply. "You can't always offer proof. Some things you have to accept on faith. While I don't primarily focus on the historical data of past lives, many cases have been presented with information that simply cannot be explained 'logically'—as we understand the word. People describe their lives and deaths in foreign countries where they've never visited, yet they know details they could only have gotten from living there."

"Couldn't they have seen a movie or TV show?" I asked, playing the devil's advocate. "Maybe they read it in a long-forgotten book."

"Perhaps," he admitted. "But how do you explain their going to a particular town or village and its obscure graveyard, reading names on tombstones that correspond to people known to have actually lived during that lifetime?"

I shrugged. "I don't know."

"We're not just a handful of believers," he stressed. "And the numbers are growing steadily. A 1982 Gallup poll showed that sixty-seven percent of Americans believe in life after death. There are more than 2,500 American bookstores specializing in books on life after death. Over twenty-eight percent of the British and twenty-three percent of Americans believe in reincarnation, but—illustrative of science refusing to believe what it cannot document—only five percent of my psychiatric colleagues believe in reincarnation."

"Why do you?"

He smiled. I sensed that he'd been asked this question before, too. "Throughout the history of humankind, acceptance of an idea or entity often lags behind the accumulation of knowledge. Information is acquired through and built upon by newer knowledge. Things can and do exist even if we don't know about them. Therefore, the 'truth' of a matter is ever changing; truth becomes a growing entity. The distant planet Pluto was in our solar system even before our telescopes were strong enough to pick it out of the heavens in 1930. America existed and was inhabited despite Columbus's peers laughing at him for sailing 'off the edge of the world.' And if we had attempted to describe the FAX machine to businessmen twenty years ago, they would have thought us deranged."

"I still don't understand how a FAX works," I admitted wryly.

"The acceptance of past lives is hardly a new idea," Dr. Klein continued. "Eastern cultures have believed in reincarnation for centuries. The Bible and the mystic writings of the Jewish Kabbalah speak of it. Voltaire is said to have remarked, 'After all, it is no more surprising to be born twice than it is to be born once.'

"Our history is replete with names of reincarnation believers—General George S. Patton, Henry Thoreau, Salvador Dali, Victor Hugo, Ralph Waldo Emerson, Charles Darwin, Mark Twain, Benjamin Franklin, George Bernard Shaw, Peter Ustinov, and Shirley Maclaine, just to mention a handful.

"What is relevant, however, is the accessing of past-life information for therapeutic use. And, as we have discovered, it works."

Despite my efforts to maintain a reporter's objectivity, I was becoming extremely interested. "How is it done? I mean, how do you actually begin?"

He smiled broadly. "I'm pleased to hear you ask that," he admitted. "Any apprehensions I held before this meeting have been quickly dispelled. You obviously have an open mind and are willing to search for new answers."

I felt somewhat self-conscious. "Well, it *sounds* crazy," I confessed, "but it also is a fascinating concept . . . so, back to my question. What happens first?"

"Well," he answered, "first I would explain to a patient about hypnosis . . . describe what happens when you are in the hypnotic state . . . Have you ever been hypnotized?"

I shook my head. "No, the only hypnosis I've actually ever seen was in the movies. Someone held a swaying watch fob or had the subject stare into a candle and the next thing you knew the person who had been hypnotized was doing something embarrassing."

"That's entertainment," he stated firmly. "Therapeutic hypnosis is not a magical art; it's a medical modality, administered by a qualified therapist. The so-called trance states you see on television or in a night club contain some erroneous information about hypnosis. Let me clear up some myths. First of all, you cannot be hypnotized against your will. You are in control at all times."

"You mean, even when you're 'under'?" I interrupted.

"Yes. If you were in the hypnotic state here in my office and the telephone rang, you would hear it."

"What else?"

"You hear the therapist's voice at all times."

"So those who say they don't remember anything while they were under . . . ?"

"Either didn't want to hear or it was suggested that they would not remember."

"Can anyone be hypnotized?" I asked.

"About eighty to ninety percent of the population can be induced into the hypnotic state."

"What about children?"

"It's easier for children. They seem less fearful."

I leaned back, staring at my notes. He kept silent, waiting for me to speak first. It was a technique I had often used when conducting interviews. If the reporter keeps quiet, usually the interviewee will fill the void, often with a good quote. Now this method was being used on me . . . and most effectively. "What exactly is hypnosis?" I asked.

"It's an altered state of consciousness," he answered. "The patient becomes relaxed, shuts out all stimuli other than the voice of the therapist, and focuses in on what is being said. Concentration is heightened. The patient relaxes even more, then goes from the fully conscious level to the subconscious state."

"Is that what I've heard called the 'trance state'?" I asked.

"Yes, that's the popular name for it. The depth of this state," he continued, "varies from light to deep."

"Like falling asleep?"

"No," he corrected. "It's important to understand that you are *not* asleep—that is, unconscious—during trance. The conscious mind monitors what transpires. That means if you, you being the patient, are uncomfortable or just desire it, your conscious mind can take you quickly out of the trance. This is why you won't behave inappropriately or do something you ordinarily wouldn't do during hypnosis. As I've said, you are not giving control over to anyone. You are in command. Interestingly, it is at this level, also known as *the alpha state*, where dreaming occurs."

"So you're relaxed, you go into the hypnotic state—then what?"

"I ask you to go back to an earlier time. Some therapists first regress their patients to childhood, then infancy, then into a past life. I prefer having my patients access a past life directly."

"This may be a dumb question," I said, "but can the person who's being regressed to a former life get 'stuck' in the past?"

He laughed. "It's not a 'dumb' question. Everyone asks that. No, I've never had anyone get 'stuck' and to my knowledge, neither has anyone else who is doing past-life therapy.

Remember, your conscious mind is aware of what's happening. You can break the trance state anytime you want to."

I was silent a few minutes. Then ... "What does it feel like? What happens when ... do you feel like you're dreaming or is it as though it's really happening? ... What about your senses? ... How do you ...?" I had so many questions I couldn't ask them quickly enough.

Dr. Klein looked at me thoughtfully. Then he grinned almost mischievously. "Why don't you find out firsthand?"

I stared at him. "You mean ...?"

"Sure," he said easily. "Try it yourself. Then you'll know."

3

First Try

CAROL

"Do you want to try it?"

He offered the challenge and let it dangle temptingly before me as he leaned back, waiting, smiling slightly as I sorted through my thoughts.

I admitted to myself that when first agreeing to meet with Dr. Klein I had somehow sensed that this probably would not be just another first interview for a "Disease of the Month" type book. I had not, however, considered the possibility that I might be investigating past-life therapy from an intensely personal vantage point, with myself as the subject. At least, I didn't think I had.

Still, I had long been an advocate of the "George Plimpton

School of Journalism"—that is, writing from experience. In order to write about soccer for a specialized sports magazine, for example, I once joined a high school soccer team and practiced against a professional soccer team. Many of my medically oriented books and articles have been written from personal experience although also heavily supported by research from experts in the particular field. Was this really any different?

How better to write about past-life therapy, I concluded, than by trying to experience it firsthand, so that I could describe to readers how it actually felt, share my fears and anxieties, furnish them with the vicarious encounter. If nothing happened, I would report that. If something did happen, if I actually were regressed into a past life . . . it was an overwhelming thought. My reporter's antenna was quivering. I smiled back at the psychiatrist.

"Let's do it," I said.

Dr. Klein excused himself to get a small tape recorder and microphone so that we could record whatever might occur. Although I felt some anxiety, I wasn't afraid. Curiosity overruled caution. The psychiatrist exuded a quiet confidence and gentleness. I felt safe. Later, my research confirmed that this sense of confidence and trust is beneficial in the therapist-patient relationship for the hypnotic state to be successfully induced.

"What if nothing happens?" I asked as he fiddled with the tape recorder, admitting that machines of any sort had never been his strong point.

He shrugged. "Then nothing happens . . ." His casual answer lifted any sense of responsibility or fear of failure I might have had. This was to be a simple experiment. Nothing more. In college I had often earned spending money serving as a guinea pig for psychology majors. This was just one more research study. Nothing to lose.

"What issue would you like to work on?" he asked.

I hesitated. It was the first— but far from the last— time I realized that in carrying out this experiment, I would be investigating my own psyche, possibly exposing my own frailties and fears. Was I willing to? And, more important, was I willing to go public with it? I quickly tried to determine how much of myself to reveal at this time. I went for the first thing that popped into my head. "How about my fear of heights?"

He nodded. "Get comfortable," he instructed after clipping a small microphone to my jacket lapel.

I wiggled in the chair, suddenly feeling a little self-conscious. I was aware of my heart pounding. First, I placed my arms on the padded arm rests, then moved them to my lap, and finally transferred them back to the arm rests again. I uncrossed my legs and stretched them out in front of me. The toes of my two-inch high heels stuck up in the air, making me giggle to myself. Absurd! I feel like the Wicked Witch in *The Wizard of Oz*, I thought. Should I take my shoes off? Leave them on? What *was* the proper thing to do when one was about to attempt a flight into the past?

"Just relax," Dr. Klein said softly, as though sensing my slight uneasiness. Unexpectedly, I felt my body relaxing as though I had just sunk into a warm bubble bath. When he asked me to focus on a spot across the room, I fixed on the gold seal of his medical degree. My eyes fluttered, felt heavy, and I heard him suggest that I might want to close them. I did so. To my surprise, it was a simple induction. No flickering candle flames to stare into, no swaying watch fobs.

"Remember that you will always be in control," he reminded me gently. "Always safe. You will be able to hear my voice..." He spoke in a soft monotone. I felt myself drifting, similar to the feeling one has just before falling asleep. It was quite pleasant.

He asked me to take a deep breath, then slowly let it out. I repeated this at his suggestion about three times. This procedure apparently calms you down to start the relaxation mechanism while it frees the mind from other thought. It begins the process of focusing.

I heard him say softly, "I'd like you to visualize yourself at the top of a flight of stairs, holding onto a banister . . . a very comfortable staircase. One that's very beautiful. There'll be twenty steps all told. When I say so, start walking down. Each step that you take you'll find yourself relaxing more and more . . . entering very easily into the hypnotic state. I'll pick up the count with you in a short while . . . Okay . . . now we're at step ten together . . . even if you haven't reached that level, we'll start walking down together. Nine . . . eight . . . seven . . . six . . . five . . . four . . . three . . . two . . . one. Okay . . . You're feeling very comfortable right now . . . very relaxed . . . At this point we're going to work with relaxing all your muscles. I'm going to mention the muscle group and you're going to focus in on it. When you do, that area will totally relax.

"All the muscles around the scalp and forehead, relaxed . . . Focus in on that. Now all the muscles around your eyes are relaxed . . . Your lips, totally relaxed . . . Muscles around your chin, relaxed . . . All the facial muscles, relaxed . . . Very good."

DR. KLEIN

Carol responded to my suggestions almost immediately. I could see her face grow slack.

I continued with the induction. "Now all the neck muscles . . . especially the back of the neck where it gets tight and tense, relaxed . . . shoulders, relaxed . . . Now you'll feel a wave of relaxation going to both elbows . . . arms . . . wrists . . . hands . . . and out the tips of your fingers . . . Total relaxation . . . Again, all the neck muscles, relaxed . . . shoulders, relaxed . . . And now the wave of relaxation is going to go down your body . . . to your chest . . . abdomen . . . hips . . . thighs . . . total relaxation . . . Now down to your knees . . . your legs . . . ankles . . . feet . . . and out the tips of your toes.

"Your body is feeling excellent. At this point I'm going to

count backward from five. With each number you'll find yourself going deeper into the hypnotic state. As I approach zero and then say zero, you'll find yourself in a deep, deep trance. You'll feel extremely relaxed . . . Five . . . four . . . three . . . two . . . one . . . zero."

She was following my suggestions beautifully and had successfully entered into the hypnotic state.

"Carol, now again we're going to use our visualization. You're going to see yourself in a garden . . . Do you see it?"

She nodded slowly.

CAROL

I inhaled, breathing in the scent of what seemed without a doubt to be gardenias. He paused as I relaxed even more. Then he continued speaking in a gentle, almost monotone voice.

"Surrounding the garden are doors, different colored doors. I want you to select one of the doors. It is through this door that you will enter a past life dealing with your fear of heights. Which color do you choose?"

To my surprise, I could visualize doors appearing through the thick ivy that covered the garden walls in my mind. But somehow, it didn't really seem strange to me at all. They were, indeed, of different colors, although dim. Only one door stood out.

"Green," I said with some wonderment in my voice. "The green door."

There was no surprise in Dr. Klein's voice. He spoke in the same confident, gentle tones as before. "I want you to go to that door and open it. Now step through the door . . . Have you stepped through the door?"

"Yes," I answered.

"I want you to look at your feet and tell me what you see."

I felt myself looking down. There was only darkness. "Nothing."

If Dr. Klein felt concerned that it "wasn't working," it was not evident in his voice and his confidence relaxed me. He just proceeded with another question. "Okay . . . Do you have anything on your feet or are you just barefoot? Do you see your feet?"

"Black shoes." I was surprised, but they were there. I could see them.

"Black shoes?" he repeated in his same low voice. "Now look at your body and tell me what you have on. Describe your clothes, if you are wearing any."

There no longer was darkness. I felt as though I was reporting objectively on a movie I was watching. "Black dress. Drop waist."

I described my hair, then followed his suggestion to look around to tell him where I was.

"Look at the terrain," he instructed, "if you're in a place . . . maybe in a city . . . see buildings . . . "

"No," I interrupted. "There's mountains in the background." I went on to describe what was playing out before my closed eyes. "Rocks . . . I'm alone . . . waiting." He asked for the year. I hesitated. Then a number appeared in my mind . . . "I want to say . . . 1116," I answered slowly. "But I don't know why."

I heard his voice, heard myself answering his questions, although I had no idea where the information was coming from. He told me we were going to a significant time in this life I found myself in, that when he counted three, I would be there. He counted, "One, two, three. Tell me what you see and what's happening," he said.

I felt my view shifting as though someone had pressed the fast forward button on the videotape I was watching.

"I see a small house," I answered. "It's stone. Dirt floor. And there's only women there."

"Are you with the women?"

"I'm . . . they're there and I'm with them," I responded. "We're the women who've been left." I described myself as young . . . eleven or twelve . . . then told him that men on horseback had raided my village. The village men had run off, the women and children had been captured. My mother had been killed by a spear wielded by one of the men on horseback. He asked questions; I answered them knowingly, corrected him when he misunderstood, repeated the same information when he asked again later, and gave specific details from what I was seeing from deep within the hypnotic state.

For some reason, I had been singled out, I told him. The other women had moved to the other side of the building they were being held captive in. I saw myself pushing open a door . . . described to him what I was doing as I felt myself doing it. I was like a television reporter, describing a scene in depth.

"I walk down a path . . . and some of those men on horses come. And they poke at me with their spears . . . " Suddenly my objectivity vanished. It was happening . . . it was happening *now* and to me. My voice cried out in childlike tones. "They're teasing me. They . . . they're pushing me toward the edge of the cliff . . . " I felt actual fear and began trembling.

"Go ahead," Dr. Klein said, encouraging me to continue describing the scene.

"And they . . . they're all around me . . . " I began to cry . . . "and they're backing me up . . . they're backing me over to that cliff."

"What's happening to you?" he asked gently.

"And . . . and I stumble . . . and they keep poking me with the spears." I sobbed, childlike, feeling real terror and confusion. "I haven't done anything to them. They're just playing with me. And they . . . " I swallowed more tears . . . "I fall over . . . I fall over the cliff."

"Okay," he said quickly. "Are you falling to your death now?"

"Yes," I answered, crying harder.

"Go ahead and cry," he told me . . . "and after you die,

your soul will leave your body. You can tell me when that happens. Go ahead . . . "

I cried softly for a few moments, then stopped. I sighed.

"What's happening?" he prompted. "Has your spirit left your body?"

"Yes," I answered as though it was the most natural question in the world.

"How do you feel now?"

"Light . . . like I'm floating." I felt myself smiling.

DR. KLEIN

Carol remained in that state for a few minutes. I interrupted the peacefulness only to ask what lessons she felt she had learned in this life and how it might be applicable to her present life. We talked briefly. I suggested that she might feel better in her present life because of her reliving the experience of falling to her death. Now she knew when and how her fear of heights began.

Then I asked her to go back to the green door, back to the comfortable garden. She could see it clearly and reported feeling very sheltered and relaxed.

"The garden is nice as before." I said it as a comment, not a question.

"Yes," she answered.

"Pleasant," I continued. "I want you to feel very comfortable there . . . It's a very comfortable place to be. A very safe place to be. There might be some white lights around you. You'll come out of this experience today and back to the present when I count to three. Each number I count upward you'll feel much more alert. You'll feel good and positive about yourself. You'll feel safe. You'll feel comfortable. Again, you'll be able to recall what happened to you during this journey into a past life. One . . . coming up. Much more alert. Two . . . coming very, very alert. Comfortable. Three . . . open your eyes . . . "

She opened her eyes and blinked. "Well?" I said.

Carol stared at me and leaned back in her chair. "Strange!" she said at last. She sat musing over what had happened to her. "Was it my imagination?" she asked. But before I could answer, she added, "But it couldn't have been. It was too real. I saw it like a movie. I felt myself falling. The panic was real . . . "

CAROL

One week later, I arrived at a vacant lot where my husband and I were planning to build a new house. The builders had erected scaffolding so that we could get an idea of the view from the upstairs.

"I told them you'd never climb up that high," my husband announced upon my arrival.

"I'll try it," I said. To both of our surprises, I scampered up the thirty-five-foot scaffolding as comfortably as if I had done it all my life. There was no fear; no anxiety. I stood on the top looking out into the bay beyond. There was a slight breeze blowing against my face. It felt good. Whatever had occurred at Dr. Klein's office had released me from my lifetime fear of heights.

4

Doubts

CAROL

"*I* have doubts."

I typed it in boldface on my computer, then leaned back, staring at what I had written on my monitor. Then I moved forward and added an exclamation point.

Once again, I replayed the scene from the psychiatrist's office in my mind. I had listened to the actual taped version so often that I had almost committed it to memory.

It must have been my imagination, I thought. Everyone's always said I have a very active imagination. That's the only logical explanation. That *has* to be what happened.

And yet... I did feel myself falling. The terror was real. There's no denying the fear expressed in my voice on that tape.

I searched for a reasonable explanation. As a writer of medically oriented books for lay readers, I'm used to sifting through research, balancing conflicting claims from professionals, and analyzing my material. I actually enjoy the mental challenge. I am well aware that many earlier medical and scientific ideas were laughed at when they originally were presented . . . claims by Galileo that the earth actually revolved around the sun, rather than vice versa, or by Semmelweis who was first to suggest that he and his fellow physicians might be able to prevent the spread of childbirth fever if they washed their hands before examining patients about to deliver.

I'm not the only one who's had this type of experience, I mused. It's happened to others as well. Mass hysteria? No, we can't all be crazy. Then I thought, I wonder how many others have experienced past lives and don't talk about it?

Just a few days after my initial visit with Dr. Klein, my husband and I attended a baby shower with friends. One of the guests was a well-respected local psychiatrist. I waited until we were alone at the buffet table.

"Tell me," I said causally. "Have you ever age regressed a patient?"

"Many times," he answered.

"Have you ever regressed anyone into a past life?"

He looked at me in surprise, then questioningly as though he wondered if I were serious or joking. At first, I thought he was angry. Then he looked around quickly. Seeing that no one was nearby, he nodded. "Yes," he said. "Many years ago. I regressed an eighteen-year-old boy in Cuba. He suddenly began to speak in Portuguese and tell me of his former life as a Portuguese marquis."

"I'd like to hear more about it," I said eagerly.

"Call me," he responded. "We'll talk in my office." Then he moved back to the safety of the group. I watched him retreat, my cheeks burning with excitement. It had happened to him as well. I was on the trail of a fascinating story.

I could feel it. This doctor had offered me the opportunity for an interview. I would take him up on it. A good reporter always finds a second confirming source—even if the primary source is herself.

A few weeks later, I took the psychiatrist up on his offer. I sat on his couch, taking copious notes as he spoke.

"It was my senior year of medical school," he began. "The year was 1947 or '48. In Cuba. There was a neighbor boy who came to me with a problem. He was shy with girls. He asked if I could help him become less shy.

"I had learned to use hypnosis, had used it on patients as an alternative to anesthesia. He seemed like an excellent subject, so my friend, a fellow medical student, and I agreed to help him.

"Actually," he said with a grin, "my thought was to see if I could hypnotize him so that he could read into the future. If he could tell me who would win at the races, I could be rich. Remember, I was very young and it all seemed like a game. Of course, nothing happened. He wasn't able to see into the future under hypnosis, although he *was* a good subject.

"My friend suggested we try to regress him, have him go backward. We tried that and got him to go back to his second birthday party. He remembered the entire party—the names of his guests, what gifts he received, everything.

"Then my friend urged me to have him go back further. I tried. 'Go back to 1920,' I said. 'Are you living?' I went back by tens. There was no response. I kept going backward until I got to 1790. 'Are you living?' I asked.

"To my amazement, the boy stiffened. 'Mission,' he said in Portuguese.

"I thought he was talking about a building. 'Where is the mission?' I asked him, answering in Portuguese, which I knew fairly fluently.

" 'Mission do rey,' he answered, which meant he was on a mission from the king. He described being a liaison between the king of Spain and the king of Portugal. He said he was the Marquis of Castillo Branco.

"Every night my friend and I repeated the sessions with this young man. We explored his former life day to day. At one point, he described being in jail in October of 1756. When, months later, I asked him again about this period of his life, he described once again being in jail.

"He told us he was a great swordsman. During a duel, he killed a friend of the king and was sent to France in exile. Telling of his life there, he spoke in a rudimentary French. As he described living there longer, his French became less tentative. Finally, he became totally fluent as over a six months' period.

"Becoming bored with this one past life, I decided to regress him still further. Once more I regressed him by ten years at a time. When I got to 1270, I asked, 'Are you living?' He grew rigid and answered, 'Ja.' He began to speak in German, a language I know almost nothing about.

"For our next session, I enlisted aid from a professor from the university who spoke German to act as translator for me. When the session was over, we went out into the hall. 'Well?' I said, 'Does he speak German?'

"The professor looked a little shaken. 'Yes and no,' he said at last. 'The boy *is* speaking in German, but it is an ancient German. It's not spoken any more.'"

I was scribbling as fast as I could. Over the years I had improvised my own brand of shorthand. "What happened to the boy?" I asked at last.

"He went to college, then law school. The strange thing is . . . remember I said he had mentioned being an excellent swordsman in his first regression?"

I nodded.

"Well, he joined the fencing team and became a champion."

"What do you make of all this?" I asked. "Could the boy have made it all up?"

"Impossible," the psychiatrist responded. "He had no

way of knowing Portuguese, let alone French and ancient German. I later found the marquis coat of arms. It was as the boy had described it. No, it was not his imagination. I have no doubt that he spoke of his actual past lives."

"Reincarnation?" I asked, holding my breath.

"Reincarnation," the psychiatrist said. "No doubt of it."

Notwithstanding this remarkable tale, I still had lingering doubts. I struggled to maintain my professional objectivity, despite the overwhelming emotions I had experienced. As was my practice when dealing with a new subject for a book or article, I turned to my computerized data base and checked the literature—both professional and lay—to see what had been printed on "reincarnation" and/or "past lives." To my surprise, there was a vast amount.

Ian Stevenson, M.D., from the University of Virginia Medical Center had researched and documented hundreds of cases of children suggesting reincarnation as the only possible explanation. Bestselling authors Dr. Raymond Moody, Ruth Montgomery, Edgar Cayce, and Dr. Kenneth Ring had published numerous books on the subject.

Although only a handful had written on the use of therapy involving past lives, I read those, too, concentrating especially on two recent publications by psychiatrist Brian Weiss, M.D., which further advanced this concept. There was no denying that the authors of these books had successfully used past-life therapy to quickly reach into the patient's subconscious and to heal.

In addition, I discovered that physicists had written scholarly volumes describing how the theory of quantum physics made past lives a plausible answer for otherwise unexplained phenomenon. To my amazement, I found believers in reincarnation in general literature as well. Baruch Spinoza, Voltaire, Goethe, Herman Melville, Leo Tolstoy, William Wordsworth, Percy Bysshe Shelley, Jack London, and Edgar Allan Poe had all written of their beliefs. So had Henry Ford, Richard Wagner, and Pearl S. Buck.

I thought about the feeling of exhilaration I had experienced standing high on top of the scaffolding on the vacant lot, looking above the trees, and feeling the breeze from the bay blowing through my hair. Something *had* happened while I was in the hypnotic state at Dr. Klein's office.

Personally, as well as professionally, I felt drawn to follow up my first foray into past-life therapy, to explore where this path would take me.

I reached for the phone and dialed Dr. Klein's number. When the psychiatrist answered, I identified myself, then hesitated for just a moment. "Dr. Klein," I said firmly. "When can we meet again?"

5

A Second Journey

DR. KLEIN

*I*met again with Carol on April 1. I could tell she was a trifle tense, so we talked a little about my daughter's graduation which I had attended the previous weekend.

When there was a natural pause in the conversation, I asked her, "How do you feel?"

"Nervous," she admitted. "I feel a little schizophrenic. It's weird trying to be objective about something when you're becoming actively involved. I feel as though I'm wearing two hats."

"You are," I responded. "But that's what makes this so interesting. You're a professional, trained to capture emotions and impressions and expose them to print. There's never been a book *by* the regressee. This is your opportunity to describe to others just what you're experiencing." She nodded. Sensing she was stalling, I asked, "Shall we begin?"

"I don't think it's going to work this time," she said. "I don't think anything's going to happen."

I shrugged. "If it doesn't, it doesn't."

"Okay. As long as you understand . . . "

Taking a legal pad off my desk so that I could take notes, I asked her to get comfortable.

She settled back into the armchair. I could tell that she still was uneasy. "Any issue you want to work on?" I asked. We had agreed earlier that as the purpose of past-life regression was to help people confront and overcome problems, we should treat our sessions as therapeutically as possible.

"Well . . . what about assertiveness? I've never been very assertive," she confessed. "I feel people take advantage of me."

"That's fine," I told her as I began the induction process. "Carol, take a deep breath and slowly let it out. Breathe in . . . that's it. Now slowly let it out. Your eyes may feel heavy and, if you wish, close them."

Her eyes flickered and closed. Despite her concern that she wouldn't be able to "go under," as she phrased it, I could tell that she was quickly entering the trance state. I continued the induction process, then suggested that she once again would find herself in the beautiful garden. As before, she viewed different colored doors, selecting the green one once again.

"I want you to pause a moment by the door," I said. "That's it. Now push it open and step through. Look down at your feet. What do you see?"

CAROL

It was as before . . . a film unfolded as I watched and reported what I observed. "Sandals," I said. "With thongs wrapping around my ankles."

In answer to Dr. Klein's questions, I described myself as wearing a smock, in a brown gauze-like material. I was a woman, in my early twenties. My name, I told him, was Gerta.

"Gerta," Dr. Klein said. "Look around you. What do you see?"

My eyes flickered rapidly. "Sand. And right here, temporary places."

He obviously didn't understand. "What do you mean, 'temporary places'?"

I made a face and shook my head, frustrated by his seeming inability to grasp my meaning. "Temporary," I repeated. "They're not really homes." I couldn't find the right words to describe what I was seeing and that lacking surprised me. "We're on route to somewhere. These are just lean-tos . . . a covering while we sleep. Shelter, really. We're in the middle of a journey. There are many of us. I think we're prisoners. My hands are tied to other people."

"Are you with anyone, Gerta, or are you alone?"

Again, with closed eyes I searched. "No, no family. I think I'm an orphan. I've been raised by others." Then I noticed something and added in surprise, "There are no men . . . just women and children."

He asked what land this was and I called it "Persha" and named the year as 65. "Has Jesus been born?" he asked. I shook my head no.

Dr. Klein then suggested we go to the end of this journey. I described being taken to a city with houses built of sand or clay within the walls.

"We're put into a holding area," I explained. "I think we're being sold as slaves. Three women and I are brought out together. The others cry; I do not. A fat sweaty man buys us, and we're taken to a Moorish-looking house in a cart. A woman takes us to a pool and bathes us. She talks . . . but I can't understand the words. I can only guess at what she's saying. We're given white gowns to wear and are locked in a room to sleep. I am so thirsty. There is a jug of water and some fruit for us. There are mats on the floor. The floor is made of stone... broken rocks with the flat side up." I could feel the texture. I smiled.

"It feels so cool," I told him. "So good on my feet. I don't think I've ever felt a floor before."

DR. KLEIN

Carol's eyes moved rapidly as though she were viewing a movie. "The next morning the woman lines us up and begins talking," she related. "I think she is giving instructions, but I don't understand what she is saying. The other three seem to speak her language, but I don't." Carol frowned, showing her frustration. "She takes me to a young woman and shows me how to dress her, do her hair, and such. My mistress is good with me and patient, although I often don't understand what she is saying. Sometimes she becomes impatient and pushes me, but we get along. I sleep beside her bed on a mat."

Abruptly Carol grew silent, as though reflecting on her life with this young woman. I moved the scene along for her by suggesting it was two years later. "What is happening?" I prompted gently.

"My mistress is married. Her husband makes advances to me when she isn't around. I try to ignore him because I don't want to do anything that would hurt her. I like this woman and she trusts me. He is persistent and I try to fight him off, but I'm afraid to tell him no. He..." she hesitated, as though reluctant to share this information. "He . . . 'takes advantage' of me. I'm worried that my mistress will find out and be disappointed with me. I wouldn't hurt her for anything."

Without pausing, she continued to describe to me her helpless betrayal of the young woman who soon discovers what has happened. Angered, Gerta's mistress orders her to be put to death.

"I'm taken out to the courtyard. It's full of big boulders.

It's filled with rocks. The mistress is watching from her window and everyone from the house . . . all the servants . . . are brought out. They pick up stones and they're taking off my dress. I'm naked. They pick up rocks to throw. At first, I try to dodge them, but they keep coming from all directions . . . they keep coming." Carol shifted slightly in the chair as though trying to avoid being hit. Then she smiled slightly. "'It really doesn't matter,' I say and I stop trying to elude them. They hurt at first, but then I stop feeling any pain. I just feel sad about my mistress. I really was fond of her."

"What happens now?" I asked.

Carol hesitated a moment and then began talking with a surprised tone in her voice. "I feel myself being drawn up, as though I'm on my back in a pool floating and someone is pulling me along in the water. I look down and see what's left of my body." She shook her head sadly. "It's pulverized. There's no face, just a bloody pulp. But I feel at peace as I'm lifted up. The lights are bright. There's someone with me, in back of me, hugging and loving me. I feel cared for. I don't see a face. It's hidden. Just a form in a brown robe."

"What do you feel?"

"Peaceful . . . love . . . it's so beautiful."

"Now that you're in this 'in-between' state," I said, "let's converse about what happened . . . What have you learned during Gerta's life?"

"That I need to speak up . . . learn the language. I should have said no to the young woman's husband. They can't kill me twice."

"What have you learned that can help Carol in her present life?"

"To assert herself," she answered firmly.

"Was there anyone in Gerta's life whom you know in your present life?"

Carol looked around, eyes still closed. Then, with surprise, "The young woman. I think she is one of my daughters."

I directed her to return to the garden. She hesitated for a

moment, then followed my suggestion, and I brought her out of the trance state.

CAROL

"I really didn't want to go back to the garden," I explained to Dr. Klein as soon as he roused me from the trance state. "It was so peaceful where I was that I wanted to stay a while longer." I paused for a moment, enjoying the warmth I had experienced, then shifted into my more "objective" mode. "It's hard to believe what I saw. I actually looked down and observed my body from above. I felt sorry for what had happened, but no emotion. It was just a body. I also actually saw my guardian angel. I've always sensed its presence, but this is the first time I ever saw it."

"What else stands out about this life?"

I grew thoughtful, wanting to be as explicit as I could. "The richness of details," I said at last. "My tactile senses were especially sharpened, such as feeling the coolness of the tile beneath my feet."

DR. KLEIN

Then, as is my practice, we spoke of the practical applications of the past-life experience. In this case, it was Carol's obvious need to speak up and become more assertive. As Gerta needed to "learn the language" of the people she was serving and speak out for herself, so Carol needs to "learn the language" as well.

"You mean if Gerta . . . gee, that seems strange to call myself that," Carol laughed, "if Gerta had spoken up to her mistress she might have been believed?"

"She might have," I acknowledged. "Then again, the mistress might have become so angry that she would have ordered Gerta to be killed anyway. But as you said, 'You can't be killed twice.'"

We talked in greater detail about Carol's past-life experience. She left, promising to research the facts that had evolved.

CAROL

As I examine the data that surfaced during this past-life sojourn, I feel as though I'm both the defense and prosecuting attorneys in a trial case. Part of me wants the information to be correct in order to validate the experience, while the other half wants "proof" that it's just the overactive imagination of which I've often been accused. Yet much does check out as accurate.

I discovered, for instance, that the Egyptians *did* war against the Persians. It was called "Persis" then, not "Persha" as I, or rather Gerta, originally said. Now it's known as Iran. There were many languages spoken at that time, so it's very possible that Gerta would not have spoken the tongue of her captors.

In addition, drawings of the houses of that era show them built into the walls as "Gerta" described. Many nobles lived in stone houses.

On the negative side, the 65 B.C. date seems inaccurate.

Dr. Klein had suggested that I begin to keep a journal, in order to record my emotions and personal experiences following each meeting. Usually I'm not much of a diary person. Typically, with journals in the past, I begin with enthusiasm on January 1 and by Ground Hog's Day have either lost interest or the diary itself. However, this time I agreed to give it a try and be more diligent. My notes after this session include the following:

"Since this regression I find myself speaking up in my own behalf, reflecting afterward that it might have helped Gerta if she had done so as well. The realization or understanding gained through that past-life experience has made me more aware of my need to speak up. I actually take pleasure in the discovery of how easy self-assertion is . . . and (surprise of surprises!) that no one 'gets mad' at me for doing so.

"Recently, I was in a situation where I was unable to change my plans to carry out an errand. In the past, I would have given in and made the necessary adjustments. This time I stood firm. The other person involved said, 'Then *I'll* just do it myself.'

"This is the typical contest we two have played for many years. Now, however, I seem to have 'learned the language' of this game and was able to speak out. 'Okay. That's great,' I said. *I* won for a change. It feels good!

"I've had other 'assertiveness training' classes in the past that didn't seem to trigger any alteration in my behavior. This past-life experience, however, seems to have made an important imprint. I feel different; I'm expressing myself more confidently; it works."

6

Assertiveness:
The (Subconscious) Mind Knows Best

DR. KLEIN

One week later, Carol and I met again. At this point we had agreed to schedule regular meetings on Wednesdays at 2:00 p.m. Although I could tell that she was still struggling between two realities—what she had experienced and what she intellectually "knew" could be or not be possible—she was, nevertheless, open to new understanding and possibilities.

For my part, I was becoming very excited with what had been accomplished. Carol was a good hypnotic subject. She not only was able to quickly go into the trance state, but because of her reporter's training, she also was able to focus on details and verbalize what she was experiencing. Afterward, during what became our "debriefing sessions," she asked pointed questions, reflected honestly on what she had seen, and was tireless in researching the literature to see what others had written.

In fact, Carol had begun to read so much that I asked her to desist temporarily. "I don't want you to become 'contaminated' with other data at this time," I said. "Let's just concentrate on you and your experiences. Perhaps we should go slower so that you can assimilate all that's happening."

"No," she exclaimed. "I'm fine. Let's continue while we have the momentum."

I was pleased with her response. I, too, was fascinated with the process. Although I had regressed many patients into past lives, this was the first time that I had received analytical responses from the subject who indeed *was* wearing two hats, those of "subject" and "reporter."

"Let's try to focus on a specific issue," I said, adjusting the microphone.

She nodded.

"Anything special?"

Carol hesitated. "I'm wrestling with how much of myself to reveal," she said honestly. "It's a little scary."

"Do whatever's comfortable for you."

"Maybe . . . maybe a personal relationship . . . "

I waited. Sometimes silence is the best response. I could see she was struggling to decide how much to share with me.

"I . . . I have some difficulties with a relative . . . my sister . . . our relationship. She's controlling." She paused as though needing to bolster herself to make a decision. Then, "I'd like to work on that problem."

"Fine," I said. "Let's begin."

Carol went quickly into trance. Yet when I suggested that she select a door to lead her out of the safe garden and into a past life, her eyes searched and then a puzzled look came over her face.

"I don't see any doors," she said. "There's only ivy growing along all four walls."

So much for skeptics who say the subject always follows the therapist's suggestions. Carol was demonstrating classic resistance. Although she had professed being "ready" to discuss a personal problem and consciously *wanted* to do so, she obviously was not quite ready subconsciously. I sensed her becoming panicky.

"Don't worry," I said gently, knowing there are several ways to handle resistance. "That's all right. Carol, what I'd like you to do now is to go to an elevator . . . Are you there? Step in and press whatever button you wish . . . What button are you pushing?"

She hesitated, then answered, "Eighteen."

"All right," I responded. "When the elevator reaches the eighteenth floor, you can step out and enter into a past life." I paused, giving her time to visualize this. "Have you done so?"

"Yes."

Now we were back on track. "Look down and tell me what's on your feet."

"Boots. Brown leather boots."

"Look at your body. What do you see on your body?"

"Breeches," she replied. "Sleeveless weskit and a . . . blousy shirt."

She went on to describe herself as a man named Arad, a hunter who lived at the edge of a forest in England. I asked her to go to her home, to describe it to me.

"It's made of stone," she announced without hesitation. "It's ah . . . one room, with a loft upstairs. It's our bedroom. We go up on a ladder. There's a . . . fireplace downstairs and the floor is stone. There's hooks to hang things up on."

She went on to describe Gretchen, Arad's wife of thirteen years, who worked in the kitchen of the nearby castle.

"Whose castle is it?"

"Edward . . . Edward of . . . of something."

"I'm going to count to three," I said, "and it will come to you. One . . . two . . . three . . . Edward of . . . who?"

"Tirus," she said quickly.

When I asked the year, there was a long pause.

"It's the sixteenth century . . . 15 something. I don't know." In answer to other questions, she described her life as the hunter, Arad. "I bring in the pheasants . . . and partridge."

I asked her to go to a very significant time in her life as Arad. Her face changed. "What's happening?"

"They've come to our house," she whispered. "Someone's told them that I've kept some of the . . . some of the hunt. They're going through the house and they're looking. They don't find anything, but . . . They take us outside and hold us. They light the roof. It's thatched and it catches quickly."

"Go ahead," I urged. "What happens next?"

"They take us back to the castle and we're separated. I hear . . . I hear Gretchen screaming. I don't know what they're doing to her, but they're hurting her. She screams and . . . and . . . and I'm . . . they come for me. They say she's told. I don't know if she's told or not. I don't know if she's alive or dead. Then they take me down into this dark room. There . . . wasn't that much that I took. I don't know who told. They lay me on this table and chain my hands and my feet. I . . . I don't know . . . I don't know if they know or not. They lower this big stone. I can feel it on my chest and they keep saying, 'Did you steal?'"

Carol was breathing heavily at this point. I watched her carefully, knowing from our previous discussion that she had a preexisting asthmatic condition. If necessary, I was ready to take her out of this stressful situation at any time.

"'Did you steal?' they ask me," she continued. "'Did you take it?' and I don't say anything. They let the stone go farther. It's . . . it's . . . it's so heavy. It's hard to breathe . . . "

Now she was panting, straining with each breath.

"I . . . I say, 'It was only two grouse . . . it wasn't . . . only two grouse . . . ' and they . . . they don't lift it and . . . it's . . ." She was beginning to gasp for breath. I was ready to move her on.

"It's . . . "

I cut in quickly. "Arad, if this is the time that you're going to die, go ahead and let your soul lift. It's time for your soul to leave your body. Just tell me when it occurs . . . "

The pain left her face. Her breathing returned to normal. She nodded. "Uh . . . uh . . . " Then, faintly, "I see the . . . I look down and . . . they've crushed him."

"Where are you now?" I asked. "Where is your soul now?"

A smile crossed Carol's face. "I'm being pulled toward the light and there's Gretch waiting for me. It's Gretchen. They've killed her. But she's there, waiting for me."

She described other people waiting for her as well, including a baby they had lost. "It's very peaceful," she murmured. "We're safe wherever we are."

"What lessons?" I asked. "What lesson did Arad learn in his lifetime? What lesson was there to learn?"

"Maybe if he had confessed, they might have spared his wife."

"How is that lesson applicable to the life of Carol?"

"Not to wait so long to speak out."

We talked a bit as she "floated" in this in-between state. Then I asked, "Is there anybody else with you now?"

"There's a figure," she said. "It's tall . . . hooded, so I can't see its face." She described the figure as wearing a robe, like a monk's. "But it's translucent. Shimmers and . . . although I don't see a hand, I feel he's touching me . . . on my shoulder. Holding me. Protecting me. Don't see a face. I don't see hands or feet. But he's . . . "

"Can he talk to you?" I said. "Ask him something."

"I ask if he's always with me," she answered. "He says, 'Always as you need me.' It's a deep voice."

"Could you ask him his name?"

"He says, 'You know my name.' But I don't."

"Does he say anything else?"

"No," she sighed. "He shimmers and . . . disappears as I look at him. From the bottom up."

"Is he still there, though?" I ask. "Does he have anything else to say? Any message?"

"He's . . . 'Care . . . Guard wise.' He's nodding," she related. "I don't know what he means. I just see light. Don't see him . . . just . . . "

Sensing that we had accomplished all we were going to, I directed Carol back into the elevator, back from the eighteenth floor to the garden, where I brought her out of the hypnotic state.

Opening her eyes, she sat still a minute, collecting her thoughts. "Why didn't I see any of the doors this time?" she asked. "What happened?"

I smiled. "Resistance."

"Resistance?" she repeated. "But I don't understand. I was ready to discuss the relationship with my sister."

"You *thought* you were ready," I corrected. "But your subconscious mind wasn't ready."

"Why not?"

I shrugged. "Who knows. Maybe you need to feel more comfortable with me, with the process of regression. Maybe you aren't ready to talk about really personal issues just yet. Don't worry. It will come. Let's talk about what *did* occur."

She nodded, although I could almost see her mulling things over in her mind. "Well," she began, "Arad was most vivid to me. I could actually feel the upper arm strength that he, as an archer, had. I knew the touch of the bowstring quivering against my forearm . . . "

"Have you ever done archery?" I asked.

She shook her head. "Never . . . not in *this* life." Then she chuckled. "I'm beginning to believe this stuff!" She sobered. "It's hard not to believe it. I felt the bowstring . . . here." She pointed to a spot on her inner arm. "If you had asked, I could have described the birds I killed."

"Actually," I said, "your use of the word 'grouse' appeared quite spontaneously in your description. Do you know what a grouse looks like?"

Carol thought for a minute. "No, not really. I think it's a small game bird . . . maybe a fat chicken . . . but I'm not sure. But Arad knew."

Before I could ask her another question, she added, "And the sounds of Gretchen's cries also were vivid. I could smell the scent of sweat and fear as they dragged me down to the cellar where I was chained to the table. My chest hurt . . . it still does," she said in surprise.

"You were gasping for breath," I told her. "That's why I decided to move you on to your death. I didn't want you to suffer . . . "

"I couldn't take in enough air," she recalled. "It was a panicky sensation."

CAROL

Each time I listened to the torture part in the audiotape over the following days, I relived the experience in my memory and felt distinct anxiety. I could feel my chest tighten as Arad described being crushed by the boulder being slowly lowered onto his body.

Arad's life seemed to reemphasize to me the importance of speaking up and out, defending myself in this life. I have found myself spontaneously doing this on a few occasions since this regression and then smiling to myself, reflecting that it was Arad and Gerta who helped me do so.

The vision I had of the guide continued to trouble me . . . partly because I don't understand the message and partly because I do feel—and always have felt—myself being guided in my present life as well. Perhaps I need to become more open visually or auditorially to comprehend more.

I noted in my journal that . . . "I look forward to my next

session with Dr. Klein . . . although I feel some anxiety as well. The unknown always is frightening. I don't know where this path is leading me. I'm not afraid of stumbling; I've fallen on my face before. I think my fear centers more on finding myself alone, isolated with my discovery."

7

RESISTANCE

DR. KLEIN

As was becoming our routine, Carol and I began this week's session by discussing the continuing and lasting changes she had noticed in her behavior.

"I really seem to have lost my fear of heights," she declared happily. "We went to Disney World and rode on one of those wild rides. I've always avoided them before, but if I *had* gone on them, I certainly would have closed my eyes. This time I was wide-eyed and really had fun." She grew thoughtful for a moment. "I hadn't realized how timid my phobia had made me about trying new adventures."

"Anything else?"

"I certainly seem to be more assertive. Sometimes it

scares me because I don't want to become aggressive."

I laughed. "You've got a long ways to go before you have *that* worry."

"Will you tell me if I do?" she insisted, still unconvinced.

"I promise."

Carol shifted a bit in her chair as though she were a little anxious.

Sensing her uneasiness, I said, "Describe what you're feeling."

"I don't know. Well . . . I guess I do," she admitted. "I'm still uneasy about what might occur during a regression . . . not that I'm frightened something may happen to me," she went on hurriedly. "More . . . what will come out of it, what I'll learn about myself, what I was . . . what I am . . . Too much self-discovery, perhaps?"

She added the latter question somewhat jokingly, but I sensed a serious component underneath.

"Do you remember the thoughts you wrote in your journal last time?" I asked.

She nodded.

"What were you referring to by, 'I think my fear centers more on finding myself alone, isolated with my discovery'?"

Carol grew pensive. "*That* dealt with the fact that I'm beginning to realize that my convictions are changing, are now contrary to the mainstream. While I don't mind being considered 'different,' I don't want to be perceived as 'weird.'" She smiled, but her eyes looked troubled. "I've always tried to be honest with myself. I know that I *do* accept what I'm experiencing to be true. But my background as a medical writer cries out for 'scientific proof' and, of course, there isn't any. My entire belief system has been challenged." Her voice trembled a little and she paused to regain her composure. "That leaves my equilibrium a little shaky just now, I guess. The apprehension I discussed in my journal centered around that." She leaned back, as though exhausted by her revelation.

"I understand," I told her, "but I feel that something else is going on. Is that a possibility?"

She sat, thinking, then nodded. "It scares me," she began slowly. "What if whatever I discover traumatizes me . . . is so awful . . . "

"How's that?"

She sighed. "It wouldn't bother me if I learned I was a thief in a past life . . . or somebody horrible . . . but what if . . . "

"Carol," I interrupted gently. "You're telling me what *wouldn't* bother you," I said. "What *is* bothering you?"

She looked away as though unable to face me with her fears. She bit her lower lip, then cleared her throat twice. At last she spoke. "What if my discovery changes me so much that I become a different person? What if I can't handle it, can't cope with this new knowledge?"

Sensing the seriousness of Carol's thoughts, I took my time to respond. "My goal is to help you improve; resolve the issues, work through the problems and, as you've already experienced, eliminate troublesome phobias. You won't become a 'different person,' but rather a healthier one. Knowledge, used correctly, effectively, is beneficial. The bottom line is resolution of your problems."

"That makes sense," she said slowly. The objective reporter was back in place.

"Are you ready to begin again?" I asked.

She hesitated only a moment. "Sure. Why not?"

"What issue would you like to focus on?"

"I'm still struggling with my relationship with my sister," she admitted. "I'd like to know why I always feel so defensive with her."

"Okay. Let's give it a try." She settled into her chair and the induction was as before. She seemed not to go as deep as previously, but settled into a medium trance state. "What do you see when you look down at your feet?" I asked her.

She hesitated. "I don't see anything. It's dark."

"It's dark? Okay . . . just walk away. As you go a little ways forward, look around. What do you see?"

She paused for a long time. Then . . . "Blackness."

"Is it the blackness of night?"

Carol shook her head. "I don't think so. There's no shadows."

Once again, Carol was resisting the issue she herself had specifically requested we work on. It was the same issue we had encountered resistance with before—her relationship with her sister.

Obviously, my usual technique wasn't working. She was resisting "seeing" anything in this past life. Remembering the specific tactile details in her life as Gerta when she described the coolness of the cold tiles beneath her bare feet, I decided to focus on her sense of touch.

"Do you feel your limbs as you're walking?" I asked.

Her face grew intent as she concentrated. "Yes," she said at last.

Success! If we had remained at an impasse, I was prepared to try her other senses to see if they would pick up the trail. "Okay, take hold of your wrist. Do you have any jewelry on?" I waited.

"Yes," she answered.

"Can you tell me what that jewelry is?"

"Wide . . . wide band.

"What arm is it on?"

"The right," she answered. We had broken through her resistance. She was "seeing" once again.

"Put your hand to your head," I suggested. "Do you have long hair? Short hair?"

"It's short. It's . . . it's tight. Tight curls."

Carol proceeded to tell me that she was barefoot and a young girl in her late teens. Looking around, she determined that she was surrounded by trees and vegetation.

"It's a jungle," she announced.

I suggested she would go right to her home. Instead, she shook her head.

"There's nothing left of it," she said sadly. "Someone's been there. The main fire's been put out . . . It's smoking. I see all the houses have been destroyed. There's nobody left."

"How do you feel right now?" I asked.

"Lonesome."

I advanced her in time. She described going to another village where she was taken in by an older couple.

"What's the name of the village?"

"I don't know . . . but there was . . . there had been a baby back in the old village that I'm looking for. I wonder if maybe he's here, too . . . but I don't know what he looks like anymore. They . . . they have a lot of people who came to this village from others that also were destroyed or vacated. I don't think they moved on without me."

"Who destroyed the villages? Who were the people who did this?"

Carol shook her head. "I don't know. No one ever says. But I feel like such an outsider . . . "

"Why?"

"They're good to me. I care for them, but they can't seem to love . . . I don't know how they feel about me."

She said her name was Muwanda, that the land was in the Congo. I wanted to explore what had happened to the 'lost baby,' but first decided to have her go to a time that was very significant to her. To my surprise, she began talking about the baby on her own.

"I'm twelve or thirteen . . . " she said, her eyes fluttering as though she were watching a movie. "I was . . . I was watching the baby. It was back at the old village."

"Okay. Start again and tell me what's happening."

"I . . . I laid him down in some bushes . . . and went into the river to play. To swim. He was hidden under the bushes. And . . . I didn't think it was that long. When I came out, he wasn't there." She continued to describe what was happening in a flat, unemotional tone. "Maybe some . . . something . . . an animal . . . took him away. But he was gone and I couldn't find him. Maybe that's why they left the village. They left me."

"Who left you?" I asked.

"Everybody," she said sadly.

"Did they leave you because you lost the baby or . . . "

"No," she replied in a childlike voice. "I didn't think they knew."

"So they weren't attacked?"

"No. I think they left."

Oddly enough, she had lied to me earlier, covering up the loss of the baby by saying her village had been destroyed. I decided to follow up on this interesting development.

"Why would they leave?" I asked her.

She shook her head sadly. "Because I had lost the baby."

"Whose baby is it?"

She hesitated a long time before answering. "I think it was my brother."

"What about your mother and father?"

"They're gone. Maybe the old couple in the new village . . . maybe they know and that's why they can't love me."

I decided to try to uncover another significant event in this life, to see if it tied in with the baby in any way. "Muwanda, what we're going to do now is to go to a later time in your life . . . maybe in your later teens . . . maybe adult, whatever . . . a time . . . some time that is very significant to you. I'd like you to be Muwanda during this period, so you're reliving these experiences." I counted to three . . . "What's happening, Muwanda?"

"I've been taken as a wife by the chieftain of a neighboring village. I'm not his only wife, but I'm one of them. He's . . . he cares for me. He doesn't know about the baby."

There it was again. The baby. "How old are you now, Muwanda?"

"Twenty-four."

"Do you know what happened to the baby? Did they ever find the baby?"

"No," she answered in that same unemotional voice. "I think an animal must have taken him away. But . . . one night I tell my husband about the baby and he holds me anyway. And he says, 'Many things happen that are not our fault.' And he . . . he forgives me."

"Muwanda, can you tell me what you have on right now? Describe to me what you're wearing." I was trying to pinpoint some details so that we could determine the time period and locale.

"It's a shift. It's long . . . it's sleeveless, but it covers my whole body. My hair is long and braided and up on my head."

"What color is your skin?"

"Brown."

"Do you have any jewelry on?"

"I have a necklace. It's made of chain and it's . . . it's got a round . . . like a plate. It has his crest. It means I'm one of his wives."

She said the name of the village was Motoi, in the inner part of Africa, what they used to call the Congo. The year, she said, was 1806. I moved her along to the time just prior to her death. "How old are you, Muwanda?"

"Sixty-two."

"Where are you?"

"I'm in a hut, lying on a mat. I have a heaviness, from a bite or something. It's an infection and they use leeches to try to draw out the poisons. They put them on my chest, my sides, and my arms, because they think the infection goes from your arms into your chest."

"Is there anything you'd like to say about your life, looking back at it?"

She thought a moment. "I was lonesome for a long part of it . . . but the last part was happy. I outlived all the wives and my husband."

She seemed tired. "Okay," I said. "Allow your soul to leave your body. Let your spirit enter the in-between state. Just tell me when that occurs."

"I can see the body lying on the mat and I'm above it. I'm floating. It's . . . and there's . . . there's someone there with arms outstretched to welcome me."

"Who is it?"

"I don't know. But they . . . I feel their love. They love me and they want me and I'm safe."

"How are they dressed?"

"Tall. With robes like a choir robe . . . and I see hands, but the sun is shining on the face and I can't see a face. But the hands . . . hands have long fingers and they're beautiful. And it was worth the wait."

"While we're here right now . . . this in-between state . . . can you tell me what lesson Muwanda learned in her life?"

"I think to keep traveling. The trip is what's important and the reward is at the end, so not . . . not to stop, but to keep traveling until you get where it is."

"How is this applicable to the life of Carol?"

"I guess not to wait around for approval from those who can't give it. To keep going . . . doing your best . . . because you eventually find what you need."

"What's that?"

"You eventually find the approval. If not here, then there. But not to wait so long in one place."

"What was the purpose of Muwanda's life?"

"She cared for the old people . . . she was a good wife, too, but he had other wives. Maybe the purpose was making the trip."

I decided to ask about the baby who seemed so important in Muwanda's life. "What did the baby represent to Muwanda? The baby that was lost."

"He was . . . he was a responsibility, but I don't sense that . . . don't sense that he was . . . he was . . . that there was any emotion there. He was just part of what she carried around. Didn't resent it . . . but there was no feeling there."

"Okay. Is there anybody else where you are right now?"

She nodded. "Only this . . . this figure standing behind

me. Not protecting me, not holding me, but . . . just keeping me company."

"Does he want to talk to you or you to him? Does he want to say anything to you?"

"No," she sighed. "I just sort of feel like I'm home at last." With that she grew silent. I took her back to the garden and brought her out of the hypnotic state.

We talked about the baby, how she had a sense of loss, but without any emotion. "You had a strong sense of responsibility," I threw out casually to see what she would say.

Carol teared up. "I still do," she whispered. "I guess I feel an obligation not to 'lose the baby,' my sister, in this life, too. It's a heavy weight."

The failed responsibility of Muwanda to the baby was now reflected in Carol's present life. The feelings she had toward the baby were similar to ones she now holds toward her sister. Although also feeling responsible for many others in this life, it is this obligation unfilled from Muwanda's past that directs Carol to feel a need to care for and protect her sister. This, at times, becomes overwhelming and unrealistic.

Uncharacteristically, Carol made no journal entry concerning this regression. Still resisting, I told myself. It would come, I knew. Perhaps from another past-life experience.

8

Reactions from Others

CAROL

*T*omorrow I meet with Dr. Klein again for our regular
weekly session. Before we get together, however, I need
to organize my thoughts, to sort out data in order to know
what questions to ask—of myself, as well as of Dr. Klein.

If this were any other nonfiction book I was researching,
I'd have file boxes filled with multicolored 5" x 8" index
cards—green for quotations, blue for background material,
and pink for questions to pose to experts in the field. In this
instance, however, many of the questions must be asked of
the writer/researcher—me.

If I had to do it over again, would I still have said yes when
Dr. Klein called? Absolutely. For two good reasons: First, my

blatant curiosity would have made me accept his offer; and second, I feel that there was a reason for me to become involved at this particular time in my life. There was no way that I could have told him no. Not that it was "fated." I still had the power to determine yes or no. But somehow I must have sensed my need for a change of direction—and I've certainly begun that.

I know that I've changed since becoming involved in past-life therapy. One question is, are the changes obvious? Have others noticed? The only way to find out, I guess, is to ask.

My friends—nonwriters all—are used to my becoming involved in what they consider to be "strange" subjects as well as conventional ones. I have written about loggerhead turtles and turkeys, contact lenses and lying, diseases of the hand and heart, anorexia and acne, poisoning and periodontal surgery.

But I find myself uncommonly hesitant to talk about this project. When asked by friends about what I am now working on, I stall, self-conscious. Like a reluctant wader, I stick in one cautious toe, testing the waters of their belief.

"I'm working with a doctor," I begin, as though to make it more acceptable by billboarding *his* credentials. "A psychiatrist," I add for extra credibility. If they still appear interested, I offer, "On past-life therapy."

Friends usually react in one of two ways: Either they say, "Oh . . . " and begin to discuss "safer" subjects, like politics, religion, or our NFL football team . . . or they stare back, pause, and state with studied casualness, "I've often felt that *I've* had many previous lives."

The latter group often surprises me. Sometimes, as couples, they also surprise each other, revealing that often in marriage we don't really share everything. At dinner, one evening, I told our British friends about this project. Specifically, I described my experience as Arad, the hunter in England, who was put to death for stealing two of the birds meant for the master.

"You were a man?" my male friend asked in astonish-
ment. "Balderdash." (He actually said that.) "Even if I believed in reincarnation—which I don't—I could never
accept that you once were a man."

His wife sat quietly through his monologue, then spoke
up. "But there could be something to it. Remember that
strange sensation that came over me when we visited the
castle in France? I felt a horrible feeling of dread, as though
something awful had once happened to me there." Later, in
the ladies room, she confided that she had often thought
back to that strange experience in France and sensed that
she could have remembered more from the past if she
hadn't been so frightened by it all.

Others—acquaintances more than close friends, really—
seem to "find" me as though drawn. One came up after a
meeting.

"I had the strangest dream about you last night," she said.
"You were standing on top of a mountain, a tall man dressed
in a robe. You were talking to all of us below. I don't remember what you said, but it seemed important."

I stared back at her without speaking. Finally, I smiled. "I
had the identical dream last night. I mentioned it to my
husband this morning."

Conversations about reincarnation, past lives, past-life
therapy, and similar subjects seem to pop up constantly,
with people turning to me and saying, "You're a writer. What
do *you* think?" When I admit that I not only believe in them,
but also have experienced past lives, they often nod as
though needing and accepting the confirmation.

There seems to be a growing acceptance of past lives here
in the West. It's nothing new, of course, for Eastern cultures.
But it is a subtle change for us. I don't think it's just that I'm
more attuned to it, although that could be part of the explanation. But recently, I've noticed more comments about reincarnation and past lives in print and television ads, and
even in popular greeting cards.

My kids, all of whom are grown, also find it interesting that I'm writing about past lives. I do think, however, that they encourage my writing about my past lives because it keeps me from having much time to interfere in their present ones.

Two of my children have expressed an interest in trying to access their past lives as well. They completely accept the fact that those former lives existed and are very comfortable in wanting more knowledge of them. When I told one of them that I felt she had been the mistress who had ordered me—Gerta—to be stoned to death, she hugged me and said she was sorry. It was a most spontaneous reaction on her part.

Although I've been writing about family issues for thirty years, I have never mentioned my offspring by name or printed anything that might embarrass them. When I realized that I was caught up in this project and felt the need to write about it, I asked them how they felt about people (that is, their friends) knowing that I was involved in this particular subject.

"No problem." "My friends think it's exciting." "Who cares?" they answered. As always, they were supportive and encouraging. Some of them were more caught up in the details of what was going on than the others, but that's been true of each one of my adventures.

My mother, always the modern woman with a curiosity herself, had only one concern. "Aren't you afraid of getting 'stuck' in one of your past lives?" When I assured her that it had never been reported despite all the researchers involved in similar projects, she seemed more comfortable and often interested.

I think my husband holds mixed views about my working on this topic. While he is supportive of my work as always, he is troubled with the concept of being able to access one's past lives, let alone even having them. He is a traditionalist by birth and background, yet was sympathetic to

the feminist movement long before it was politically correct, partly because he married a woman who always
marched to a different drummer and partly because he really believed we were true partners in our marriage.

"I don't know that I fully accept the idea of past lives," he
said hesitantly the other night, "but I have to admit that you
certainly have lost your fear of heights. And you seem more
comfortable with speaking up for yourself and your beliefs.
The therapy seems to be effective, so I guess it doesn't matter if it's really a past life or not. After all, it's our perception
that makes something real."

He hasn't ruled out trying to be regressed himself. "I'm
reserving judgment," he says. Then he always has been
more cautious. He didn't even marry until he was in his early
thirties.

"How can you prove it's true?" That's probably the most
common question I've been asked. I can't prove it, of course,
but neither can I prove that the stars are out in the day-
time—yet I know they are. I can't prove that radio waves are
in the air. I don't see them, feel them, or smell them. But I
turn my radio on and I hear sound. I can't prove that I have
a soul, and yet I have experienced my body's death in other
lives and know that my soul survived. If we are truly made
in the image of God, it makes sense—to me, at least—that it
takes more than one lifetime to purify ourselves to achieve
the goodness that our Creator intended for us.

I have experienced the sense of love and peace that
comes in the in-between state. I have known the longing to
remain in that state, but accepted that I must return, that I
had more yet to learn. I feel as though in some way I have a
purpose in all this, perhaps to use my writing to tell others
what I have experienced. There is no doubt in my mind that
I am no longer the person I was before Dr. Klein's phone call
last spring. I have changed. And, as the Kabbalah states,
" . . . a life without change is not a life worth living."[1]

I guess that's the crux of it. I don't need to "prove" that the past lives I have experienced are real. I believe them to be real; reexperiencing them has created change in my present life, has given me a sense of freedom, has helped me to cope, to heal, to love more fully.

9

Family Issues Faced . . . and Resolved

DR. KLEIN

Carol's reluctance to face family issues, even when consciously wanting to do so, became the focus of our next few meetings. She disclosed being in therapy once "to work on relationships and deal with family interactions." She showed me poetry written more than twenty years ago when she had wrestled with her feelings. They were filled with anger and frustration.

"But it didn't seem to help," she said, choking up a little. "I'm still fighting. These past-life experiences have awakened so many sleeping emotions in this life. I find myself looking forward to Wednesday and my regular session with you on the one hand. Yet on the other hand, I feel a rising anxiety with all that's evolved. The moment I drive my car off the interstate and head toward your office, my heart rate increases, my mouth becomes dry, my fingers tingle. Classic signs.

"I'm like the child timidly approaching a seemingly friendly dog. I want to reach out, actually take a few tentative steps, maybe reach out a hand. Then I dart back to safety. Two steps forward, one back. I guess it's progress."

I reassured her that it was indeed. Often, Carol became subjective and emotional as she talked about our work and how she sensed it was affecting her. Although past-life therapy was providing relief from many of her underlying concerns, in no way was she suffering from a multiple or split personality. She wasn't delusional, nor did she ever hallucinate. Functioning had always been of the highest level; in fact, she had realized many honors over the course of her career. What she was now achieving was solutions and resolutions of unwanted baggage. Slowly the pace was quickening as newfound knowledge took hold. Each swallow of success caused the hunger, not to be satiated, but rather—as a good appetizer—created a desire for more.

We talked until I thought she was comfortable. Then I asked, "Are you ready to try again?" She nodded and we began the now familiar induction process. When I asked her to look down to describe what she saw on her feet, she shivered.

"It's cold. I'm wearing soft leather boots. They're mid-calf, topped with fur. My hat's trimmed in fur, too, because it's cold."

She identified herself as a man, about twenty-five years old. I asked her to look around and describe what she saw.

"Snow . . . ice . . . uh, some trees. Mountains in the . . . it's craggy, but mostly it's ice, snow. Deep, deep drifts."

She thought it was somewhere in the Ural Mountains.

"And the year?"

"15 . . . 1525."

"Are you by yourself?"

She shook her head. "No, there's people around."

"Tell me about them."

"The women are . . . are preparing hides . . . there's children running around. The men are preparing for a hunt."

She told me she wasn't married and that she lived with the other young men.

"Do you have a close friend?"

"Yes. Chatka."

"What do you and Chatka talk about?"

"Mostly the hunt . . . there hasn't been much food. I think the snows came early."

I suggested she go to a very significant time in this life. Her eyes flickered as I counted slowly to three.

"I'm a small boy . . . about eight . . . I want to go on the hunt with my father. But he says I'm too small. I'm not strong. He takes . . . he takes my brother instead. And leaves me. I . . . I'm angry . . . so I loosen the web on my brother's snowshoes because I'm mad that he's going and they won't take me." She begins to speak faster and faster, as though someone suddenly pushed the movie she was watching into fast forward.

"The water is frozen . . . when they go on the hunt. But the webbing on my brother's snowshoes comes loose and he loses his footing. He breaks through the ice. The others . . . they go to the hole and try to get him out, but he's slipped under the ice and they can't save him."

"What happens next?"

Her voice lowers slightly. "I don't tell anyone what I did . . . I . . . I'm ashamed. The next year when my father wants me to go on the hunt, I say no."

"Is this a yearly hunt?" I ask her.

"It must be . . . it's when the water freezes so they can cross the lake to get the bigger deer. My father . . . my father makes fun of me. He . . . he calls me girl names. He takes away my name."

"What is your name?" I ask. "What did they call you?"

"Can't remember any more. Now they call me . . . girl names. Like I'm a . . . like I should stay with the girls and learn to cook. I have such fear. I don't want the others to know what I did."

I suggest that we move to another significant time in that life.

"I'm older . . . I have a wife and a son. He wants to go with us on the hunt. I tell him he's too young, too small. Still he begs to go, but I can't tell my wife why I want to leave him home. I fear the gods will take him in exchange for my brother. Finally, however, I relent and say he may come. We go and he's fine, but I can't . . . can't kill any animals because my heart is filled with fear. And the others laugh. I feel as though I failed and even my son feels my shame."

We next move to the time prior to death. "Where are you? What's taking place?"

"I've gone out alone . . . across the ice. To see if I can get my courage back. I get to the center of the water . . . I hear it cracking . . . so I take off my robe. I throw away my spear, trying to lighten the weight. But the cracks . . . the cracks are everywhere. Soon my feet get pulled down and the water's cold. It's as though my brother's hand is around my ankles; the ice does break, and it's so cold. I don't struggle because I know it's only right . . . the water goes up . . . it quickly engulfs me.

"I'm being carried aloft, above the trees. I look down and see the hole in the ice."

"Where are you now?" I ask.

"It's bright. It's as though I'm going through the ice again, but it's up, into brightness."

"Is there anybody else there?"

"There are three . . . three with robes and shining faces. I . . . I understand my fate."

Having left the body of the young man, the spirit was now in the in-between state. His name was easily recalled.

"Chaul," she answered in response to my question. "C-H-A-U-L. But they called him, 'Girl child.'

"Chaul needed to learn to wait his turn. His actions kept his father from ever accepting him. As you take, you repay . . . if not in one lifetime, then in another."

"How is that lesson applicable to Carol . . . to Carol's life?" I asked.

"To know that acceptance doesn't come in each life."

"What was the purpose of Chaul's life?"

Carol frowned. "I think . . . there was some reason for him to do what he did to his brother in order to learn. It was over his brother's body that he learned."

Before I asked her to return to the garden, I questioned if there was anybody in Chaul's life who was present in Carol's. She nodded.

"The son . . . Chaul's son."

"Who was he?"

"One of Carol's sons."

CAROL

Following this regression, I entered just two brief notations in my journal. "I obviously still feel Chaul's guilt for being responsible for his brother's death . . . " and "Reexperiencing the ice breaking awakened a forgotten memory. The water was bitterly cold. I still get chilled easily."

Subsequently, I discussed with Dr. Klein my continued yearning for acceptance. Chaul wasn't accepted by his father, nor do I feel that I have been fully accepted by my mother. Unfortunately, Chaul, who reacted in anger when rebuffed in trying to hasten his father's acceptance, caused his brother's death. I *now* understand this. I realize I have to think things through, being careful not to inflict pain even innocently. Chaul's actions inadvertently caused harm and he continued to suffer for it. I'll still try to gain acceptance, but have to accept the possibility that no matter what I do, not all from whom I wish acceptance will be able to grant it.

DR. KLEIN

I had some concerns about whether we were proceeding too fast, so the following week I decided to discuss them as soon as we got together.

"Carol," I said, "do you want to moderate our pace? I don't want to overwhelm you and I know we've covered a great deal of new material in a short period. It's a lot to absorb."

She hesitated for only a moment, then shook her head. "No. Let's keep going. The objective side of me considers this exciting research. Emotionally . . . well, I'll admit that I'm juggling a lot of new information. But I think I'm handling it okay. I trust you to ease me over any rough spots."

The trust aspect was vital. What we were doing required skill on the part of the therapist. I knew that as we continued to focus on emotionally charged material, Carol might indeed have some difficult material to process.

At my suggestion, she quickly went into the trance state. She saw herself as barefoot, wearing only a cloth wrapped around herself. There were children playing nearby. "But they're not my children," she added quickly. Then she said in surprise, "I'm black."

She told me her name was Aganda, that she had been married. To Aru. But he had been killed by an animal. She had given birth to two children, a boy and a girl, both of whom had died from a sickness. She lived, she said, in a lean-to. I asked her to go inside and describe it to me.

"Here's a sleeping mat, made of grass woven together . . . some clay pots I made when I was first married. Here's a digging stick and . . . like a blanket, an animal skin."

"The blanket's an animal skin?" I repeated.

"Yeah. The nights are cold."

"You said you made the clay bowls. How many are there?"

"Two."

"Can you tell me how you made them? The actual process?"
She nodded. "You collect the clay, take a ball, wet your
fingers, and go round and round, smoothing it. You thin one
side so you can drink out of it. Then you leave it in the sun to
harden, for two days."

We then went to a meaningful period of Aganda's life,
when she was about fourteen or fifteen.

"It is the Woman's Ceremony," she intoned. "They take all
the young women and put them into a hut. They smear
something on our faces and there is chanting. There are
drums. The old women have masks on and headpieces."

"Can you describe any of those headpieces to me?"

"Yes," she answered. "It has . . . not antlers . . . triangular
things that stick out on the sides . . . hangs down over the
forehead. There's feathers . . . and there's a large nose like a
beak. They're angry-looking masks."

"Is anything happening?"

Carol's eyes fluttered. "There's a rock at the center of the
hut . . . they take each girl there. They wash . . . they wash her
from a pitcher. And . . . I don't want to be part of it. They . . .
take off our . . . a shell . . . something sharp. They spread her
legs. They're cutting her. I want to turn, but there's people
all around . . . if I do, I'll lose face by leaving. The hut gets
hotter. It's hot in there. I hear the other girls screaming . . .
they push you forward. The screaming and the drums, it's
. . . it's frightening. I want to run. Two people hold me. They
drag me over to the rock . . . it's covered with blood. They
hold my hands down . . . and then they cut me like they do
the other girls. We sort of lie over together in a corner."

"Go on."

"I know that I wanted to run. I feel shame that I didn't
want to be part of the ceremony. I . . . I couldn't ask any of
the others if they felt that way because I didn't want them to
know my shame. They give us some kind of herbs or something to stop the bleeding."

"Do you go home now?"

Carol shook her head. "No. They give us something to drink from a pitcher . . . and we sleep. All of us. Then, in the morning, we're picked up by various men who take us back to their hut. We don't go home again."

"Whom do you go with?"

"I go with Aru," she says matter-of-factly. I make note of the fact that she spoke his name without hesitation.

"Is this a happy or sad time for you?"

"It's what's expected."

"Do you want to live with Aru?"

"He's as good as anyone else. He's good to me."

"Did you know him before he came to get you?"

She hesitated, then said slowly, "No, I don't think so."

Feeling that Aganda had told me all she needed to about this period in her life, we moved on.

"I'm leaving the village," she said. Then, in surprise, she added, " . . . by choice. I'm just walking away. I have my things in a big basket. And . . . there's bananas in the basket . . . and berries and some dried fish."

"Are you leaving for good or just . . . "

"No, I'm leaving for good," she interrupted. "I think . . . I'm . . . I have nothing left in the village and I'm just going off into the jungle."

"How old are you now?"

"I'm in my fifties. I don't seem very old . . . but I'm alone. You can't be alone, so it's the accepted practice to leave. I don't have anything to protect me . . . I don't have any knives or slings or anything else. It's just what's expected. You just walk in the woods alone. I'm not afraid."

I tried to pinpoint her location. "What's the name of the village?"

"Kritchachill," she replied. Then questioningly, " . . . Kritch-achill?"

"Is there a name for this land? This big land?"

"It's by the water. There's a river that flows near it."

"What's the river called?" I persisted.

"Just 'The Big River.' You can't see across."

"Do people call it 'The Big River'?"

"Yeh."

"Are there any other villages close to you?"

"I don't see any."

"Have you heard of them?"

"Yes, I think Aru came from a neighboring village—but I'm not to go to any of the others."

"What village does Aru come from? The name?"

She paused. "I don't know. I don't remember him as a boy so he must have come from another village."

I wasn't getting any closer to identifying the details of her location, so I asked her again about the journey she was about to embark upon. "Aganda, tell me about the walk."

"It's called 'The Alone Walk.' If you're alone . . . and I don't know if it's years or . . . " Suddenly, she frowned and looked upset. "Men don't do 'The Alone Walk.' Women do."

I had never heard of this before, but was fascinated. "What happens when you do it?"

"Probably die. No one ever comes back. There's no sense of fear. It's just what's expected."

We were now ready to approach the time of Aganda's death. "What do you see?" I asked her.

"I'm in a cave. It was cool last night and I went into the cave because it offered some shelter."

"Are you sick?"

"I think I'm hungry or thirsty because I feel very weak."

"Before your soul leaves, is there anything you'd like to tell me about your life?"

"I was a good mother. It wasn't my fault the children got that sickness. I think the water made them sick . . . It was a useful life. I had a purpose . . . but then, I lost the purpose and I took 'The Alone Walk.' You have to have a purpose."

"What was your purpose?"

"I taught the younger women. I taught them how to do things."

Aganda now approached the time of her death. I asked her to describe what she was experiencing. She began to speak calmly and I took notes to remind me of specific points. Then suddenly Aganda cried out rapidly, "There's a . . . a giant cat that leaps at me . . . "

I jumped, almost dropping my pen. I was not expecting this turn of events.

"I can feel the blood trickling down like a . . . " her breathing was heavy; "there's . . . like a flash of sun and I'm floating." She grew silent.

"How do you feel now?"

"Very relaxed."

"Now that you've reached this plane, we can talk about Aganda," I said.

"She was pleasant, helpful . . . she learned to be useful."

I asked how these traits were applicable to Carol in her present life.

"She gets along with people . . . She likes people. She has a purpose."

"What's her purpose?"

"To teach."

"Why is that her purpose? Is that what she needed to do or that she found it interesting?"

"No, I think she's been 'put there.' She's . . . she comes from . . . the line is there. She's taught and will teach and will go on teaching. That's what she's there for."

"How will she do that?"

"Different ways."

"While you were Aganda, you mentioned a purpose. Is there any other purpose you can think of for that lifetime?"

"Yes, she was a good wife and mother, but she did things that the village needed. She was looked up to and respected, but it was time to leave."

"While we're in the in-between state," I said, "is there anyone else around you? Beings? Energies? Anyone you can see?"

She shook her head. "No . . . I feel energy . . . flitting like
. . . lightning bugs . . . just there. I feel like I want to reach out
to them, but I don't think we can touch. I'm not alone.
There's . . . they're friendly. There's love. It's a nice place to
be."

Before we left the hypnotic state, I asked, "Was there anyone in this past life that you recognize in your present life?"

"Yes," she answered immediately. "The head woman in
the Woman's Ceremony."

"Who was she?"

"She was my sister."

CAROL

This regression—especially the sounds of the drums and
the scent of sweat and blood at the Woman's Ceremony—
seemed extremely vivid. I was not describing a memory; it
was reality.

I was surprised at my lack of fear or sadness on "The
Alone Walk." I was so passive. Yet, I felt at-one with myself
and had a sense of satisfaction with this life. As a result, since
this regression, I sense more of a confidence in the direction of my present life.

DR. KLEIN

The last of these three sessions took place after a week's
hiatus as we both had vacations planned. At Carol's suggestion we would work solely on the issue of her inability to
outgrow a need for approval from her mother. We had discussed working on it before, but she had not felt comfortable with the idea.

I began the induction and could tell she wasn't slipping
into the alpha state as rapidly as usual—a fact which she
later also confirmed.

When I suggested that she would see the selection of

doors, she saw nothing. I reassured her. Instead of the garden, we went to our alternate induction utilizing the elevator. She picked the ninth floor and seemed to focus her concentration, settling comfortably into the hypnotic state. When she got out, however, and looked down at her feet, she again said that she saw nothing. I sensed that she was becoming frustrated with her lack of vision.

I kept my voice gentle and patient so that she would not become agitated. "Tell me what you see."

"I don't see anything," she said sadly. "It's black."

"Walk a little farther, into the light. Now look down. What do you see?"

A smile flitted across her face as her facial muscles relaxed. "Slippers. Black slippers. My robe was covering them," she confided.

"What color is your robe?"

"Black."

"And your hair?"

She frowned, seemingly impatient with my questions. "It's black, too. Long, straight . . . black . . . I don't feel as though I'm in a body, though. I feel strange. I think I'm in the spirit state."

"Look ahead, into the light. What do you see?"

"A city. It's a modern city with modern buildings . . . glass windows, but no one is there. No cars, no people." Excitement was mounting in her voice.

I was equally fascinated. None of my subjects had ever directly entered the in-between state before, which is what I guessed was happening. "Go into one of the buildings if you're able to," I said.

"Yes, I can," she answered. "They're not façades. They're real buildings . . . but no one is inside. I don't sense that any of this is real. I'm not in a body."

"Do you see anyone? Look around you . . . Do you see . . . ?" I was asking if there were any guides or other "beings" with her.

There was no doubt that she was growing impatient with my questions. "I'm looking!" she barked. "Yes . . . there's a lake down there." Obviously, she was looking back down on earth. "An island and a small lake. There's a body . . . of a man, I think. He's dead. Something's happened to his head," she reported, unemotionally.

"Do you know his name?"

"It's Gregory," she sighed, then dismissed it with " . . . but it's not important. I'm leaving. I'm floating upward."

"Where are you going?"

"I don't know. But I'm being pulled upward. They're talking to me now. They want me to go back, but I don't want to."

"Who's talking to you?"

"The guides."

"Where are you going?"

"I seem . . . I seem to be floating upward. They want me to go back but I don't think I want to just now." She was becoming agitated, restless . . . I needed to calm her down.

"Okay. Just tell me what happens. Where do you go to?"

"They want me . . . " Her eyes began to tear up. " . . . to be reborn . . . and I don't want to go to those people . . . It's to Carol's parents."

"To whom?"

"To Carol's parents. I'm . . . to go there and I really don't want to. I feel caught up in . . . like a whirlwind . . . like I'm pulling away and I'm being pushed. And I'm not ready."

"Why aren't you ready?"

"Because it's . . . it's not right for me . . . They don't want me there."

"Who doesn't want you there?"

"Parents. They don't want me . . . " She began crying. "And I'm going to have to go. I don't want to." Now she was sobbing harder. " . . . I don't want to do this," she wailed.

"Who wants you to go?"

"My guides tell me I need to." She sounded resigned.

"Why?"

"To learn . . . "

"To learn what?"

"To learn rejection . . . to make . . . to make peace . . . to make peace with . . . to have success . . . and . . . I go."

There was a long pause. I waited, not wanting to break into what she was experiencing. Then she spoke up. "I feel chill . . . "

"You feel what?"

"Chilled . . . cold."

"Why's that?"

"There's no warmth . . . "

"Where are you now?"

"It's dark . . . but I hear loud sounds. They're yelling. I know I don't want to be here . . . but I . . . I am accepting that I am."

"Who's yelling?"

"My parents," she said sadly.

"And where are you now?"

Her eyes continued to flutter. "I still don't see anything . . . I think . . . I . . . I feel pressure . . . I think I'm . . . " She laughed self-consciously. "I feel like I'm being born.

"And there're lights . . . I . . . I see a . . . like a . . . big stainless sink in the corner. And my father's there. He's disappointed that I'm a girl. The doctor had promised I would be a boy. And my mother turns away. She doesn't want to look. She feels she's let him down, too. I . . . I don't want to be here."

I could tell that she was emotionally exhausted. I didn't want her to suffer any more pain. "Okay. We're going to take you back now . . . " and went through the process of returning to the elevator at the ninth floor.

After coming out of the hypnotic state, Carol sat quietly for a few moments. "This was really something," she said at last. "I'm glad you were here."

CAROL

This entire latter experience was the strangest one yet. I obviously was resistent to going into the hypnotic state, despite the fact that I had wanted to . . . had actually insisted on exploring this particular issue. Yet it was disquietingly different. I felt "out of body" from the beginning and never settled into a human form. There really was no sense of the person of Gregory and I felt him to be totally unimportant. I wanted to describe what I was experiencing from the in-between state.

In trying to reconstruct the experience, I realize that I didn't actually hear the guides speaking; that is, there were no voices I could identify, but I did understand their message implicitly.

I felt genuine bodily tension, an inner struggle, as it were, before agreeing to be born. I observed this tension during the birth as well as after it and felt overwhelming relief when Dr. Klein's voice told me he was taking me away from the experience.

I cannot stress just how important it is to have confidence in the person with whom you are working. It is vital to know without a doubt that he or she is in control of the situation and will not allow any harm to come to you. Past-life therapy is *not* entertainment; I have learned firsthand that it is a true form of therapy, a medical procedure, and as such can be painful and sometimes frightening. It is not a place for amateurs.

It was fairly easy to verify some of the information that came out of this regression. My mother confirmed that my father *was*, indeed, in the delivery room, which was most unusual for the late thirties. She also remembered a stainless steel sink in the corner. She added that without question I was born one month early, which conforms with my statement, "I'm not ready."

Reluctantly, my mother admitted that my father's reaction to the discovery of my sex *was* one of disappoint-ment—"bitter disappointment." Although she neither con-firmed nor denied that she had turned away, she did admit that she, too, was disappointed that I had been a girl be-cause she knew how disappointed my father was.

To my surprise, this particular regression has not made me feel "more rejected." On the contrary, I find myself feel-ing more accepting, as though I now understand the family dynamics. It all suddenly makes sense. I'm now ready to face the rejection I've felt all my life. My impression that I was neither accepted nor approved of by my mother was nobody's "fault." I was simply born the wrong sex.

I see that throughout my life, I've tried to win my mother's approval by being successful, but always felt that I failed. But now, by understanding what transpired during the last regression, I'm far less driven. I've learned to accept and enjoy my mother for who she is. I still seek success in what I do, but it now is due to motivation for self-fulfillment. A calming peace has entered my life.

10

Unresolved Issues

DR. KLEIN

"*D*o you know what I think is strange?" Carol asked me at our next meeting. "I replay the tapes of our sessions and hear traffic noises from outside the building, even the aquarium bubbling here in the room. But I'm not at all conscious of those sounds while I'm in the hypnotic state."

I nodded. "It's because your concentration is so focused," I reminded her. "The induction process narrows sensory functions one by one until you relax, tune out all other distractions, and beam your attention solely onto the voice of the therapist. It's the same thing that happens when your kids stare at the television and don't react when you talk to them, or when you drive long distances and don't remember miles of it. But you don't lose control; you can 'snap' out of it whenever you want to. Look, I'll show you."

Using our usual technique, I induced Carol into a medium hypnotic state. I told her that she would relax quietly for a few minutes. Then, after about thirty seconds, I called out, "Carol." She opened her eyes quickly in surprise. "You see," I said. "You continue to react as usual. You never lose authority."

"That's reassuring," she admitted. "Not that I've been concerned. I feel very safe, but certainly my experience last week underscored that it's comforting to work with a therapist who knows what he or she is doing. I'm also amazed," she added, "how much the *reliving* of these experiences has helped the *relieving* of . . . problems. I hate to think of them as problems . . . I mean, I didn't expect this project to be so therapeutic. But it *has* been. Therapeutic and intensely personal." She paused. "What if we were to work today without any issue, just 'free associate'?"

"Whatever you want," I said, sensing her desire to get away from some of the intense emotions she had been confronting over the past few weeks.

Carol quickly returned to a deep level of hypnosis. When I asked her to look down at her feet and describe what she had on, a process known as "grounding," she seemed surprised.

"I'm wearing clogs. Wooden clogs." She continued to detail her clothing. "I'm wearing blue pants, full at the hips. A blouse . . . white . . . puffy sleeves." Her hair, she said, was blond and short. She told me she was a twenty-nine-year-old man named Hans Geeder and saw herself as Hans at a wharf. "A fishing village. It's Goerf, in Holland . . . the southern part, I think. I see boats, a fish market . . . I think I'm a fisherman."

"Where do you live, Hans?" I asked.

"In an apartment . . . a room, really, over a store. A fish store."

I suggested that Hans might want to go into the shop. "Look around and tell me the type of fish you see for sale."

She nodded, and I could almost see her pointing out each fish as she spoke without any hesitation. "There's luffs... it's a big white fish... and picklings... eels... shrimp... There's not much left. It's late."

"Is the storekeeper a friend of yours?"

"A friend of my family's."

"Is he there?"

Carol corrected me. "It's a she. She's a widow."

"What's her name?"

"Gilda Krantz."

I wanted to obtain some physical details that might be checked later. "When Gilda sells fish, do they collect money?" I asked.

"Yes."

"Do you have any money on you?"

"No... I... I should have, but I left it upstairs."

"That's okay. Go over to Gilda and ask her if she could show you a coin."

"Okay."

"She is showing it to you?" Carol nodded. "Can you describe it to me?"

"It's round... has a hole in it... It's not gold... sort of bronze. And she has some... some paper money."

"Is there any picture or anything on the paper money?"

"There's a picture of a woman... "

"Any number on it?"

"A five."

"What about the other side of the paper money... on the other side of the picture... if you turn it around?"

"Birds."

It was time to move Hans along to another important phase of his lifetime. "Describe it to me, Hans," I said.

"I'm old... I'm in a... a grass house... not a grass house, a... it's not made of wood... it's made of twigs. I'm sitting in a chair that I made when I was younger . . . I have my grand-son . . . I . . . I'm not seeing very well, but I have him and I tell him about my fishing . . . what it was like to catch fish."

"What type of boat did you use to go out on?"

"It's a big wood boat with sails . . . and a thick hull. Had three sails . . . a rudder . . . I would go out with some of the other men. We'd go early in the morning."

"What years did you used to go out? Do you recall now? When you fished?"

"It was in the 16 . . . 1600s . . . "

"Are you a good sailor?"

"Yeah."

"Did you have to call out all of the terms . . . ?"

"I . . . I don't think so. It wasn't my boat . . . I can feel the lines from the sail. It was rough . . . used to cut my hands."

Hans was sort of reminiscing, so I gradually eased him back to the conversation with his grandson.

"When you tell him about your fishing . . . what happens next?"

"He slips . . . he starts to slip off my lap. I . . . I can't hold him. I'm afraid . . . he's only four and I don't want him to hurt himself when he falls. I just feel so weak. I can't hold him any more . . . "

"Okay . . . " I said, encouragingly.

"I know I'm dying. I'm going to miss seeing him grow up to be a man . . . "

"Are you dying now?"

"No. I'm . . . I'm just . . . I guess going into a . . . a sleep for a while. My daughter . . . Kataleen lays me on a mat . . . she shoos him away, but he won't go away because he loves me. She's crying. I want to tell her not to cry . . . I don't hurt. I'm very tired."

"Are you going to die now?"

"Yes."

"Is there anything looking back at this life that you'd like to reflect on?"

"Was a happy life. Sweet life. I did everything that I enjoyed doing."

"Good. Go ahead, Hans. Tell me when your soul has left your body and you're in the in-between state . . . go ahead."

Carol smiled in wonderment. "It's like a channel opening up in the sky. Like the wind caught the sails . . . I'm . . . going up . . . I'm . . . I don't know where I am, but it's like I'm rocking on the sea . . . so soothing . . . "

While in this plane, the lessons learned readily evolved. There was no hesitation. The responses flowed.

"To let himself be loved. And to give love. That you can't hang on to it . . . "

"Can't hang on to . . . ?"

"Yeah . . . " she said as though ignoring me. "The little fellow. He'll do all right. I would have liked to see him growing. He'll be okay."

"How are the lessons learned by Hans applicable to Carol's life?"

She seemed to stir, uncomfortably. "Take time to . . . to be with those you love. I missed a lot when I was younger. So busy fishing . . . and making a living, and I really enjoyed the time I spent with the little fellow."

"What was the purpose of Hans's life?"

"To touch . . . to touch another generation with love . . . to reach out to them . . . "

Although I knew that Carol had requested we not work on any specific issue, I felt that one had shown itself. I started to ask, "Is there something in Carol's life still unresolved that surfaced in Hans's life . . . ?"

Before I could finish my thoughts, she spoke up. "He hurried through the first part too fast. He got wise too late."

Then she grew quiet and remained silent, so I felt it would be best to end the regression.

CAROL

I felt keenly disturbed on the way home after this particular regression. I still can't put into words what it was about Hans that bothered me. He *said* he did what he enjoyed doing, yet he seemed to feel regret that something still was missing from his life. I felt strongly connected to this fisherman.

Holland has always had an allure for me. Although I have never been to the Netherlands, I have always been drawn to the Dutch artists. I needlepointed a copy of a portrait by Rembrandt and was so charmed by the works of Pieter Bruegel the Elder that I purchased two posters of his paintings. Both artists lived during or within fifty years of Hans's lifetime. I also recently became intrigued by and purchased a new book, *Daily Life in Holland in the Year 1566*, which again was close to Hans's lifetime.

My research concerning the details uncovered by the regression proved fruitful. The Netherlands did have a bronze coin with a center hole, but it was used in the East Indies Netherlands. However, according to the *World Coin Encyclopedia*, during 1600-1795 coins were struck by various cities and provinces so there may have been ones as Hans described.

Although it had seemed odd to me as I reported to Dr. Klein that I saw fishermen wearing wooden shoes, I discovered that fishermen did indeed wear wooden clogs during that period. I found that strange, because I assumed wooden clogs would have become wet in the boats.

I also learned that shrimp and eels *were* major catches as I had described. Possibly what I called "picklings" were actually herrings, as they are pickled in vinegar.

Hans's lifetime in the 1600s was during the golden age of the Netherlands. It became a major sea power. Since childhood, I have always been drawn to water. I thought it was because I was a Pisces; perhaps it is because I was a fisherman in a former life.

11

STILL UNRESOLVED

DR. KLEIN

"*I* don't like Hans very much," Carol said vehemently as we began our next session.

Her expression was so disapproving that I had to smile. "Why not?"

Uncharacteristically, her eyes did not meet mine. "Oh, I don't know. He makes me feel disconcerted . . . uneasy. Was he telling me that I had needed to take more time, give more love with those close to me early in life?"

"What do you think?" I wanted to let her work it out on her own.

"Maybe I rushed through my formative years too fast. If it's true, I want to deny this possibility. Still . . . "

94

she drifted off in thought.

"What are you thinking?"

"Just . . . well, I *did* make sacrifices for my work. Not with my kids. At least, I don't think so, although maybe I sometimes was with them only physically, while my mind was out working on reorganizing a paragraph or two. But I did knowingly sacrifice friendships when I was younger. There just wasn't enough time for everything. Something had to be heaved over the side, and I guess it was a lot of potential social life." She paused. "I never thought I had missed it before."

I found it interesting that she chose nautical terms to illustrate what she was thinking. More influence from Hans, perhaps. "What can you do about it?"

She smiled. "Well, obviously I can't do anything about redirecting the past. I can't change what has happened, can't physically recapture my lost youth. I'll have to make alterations in another time, a life yet to be lived."

As she seemed lost in thought, I sat silently for a few minutes, allowing her time to develop her ideas. We had definitely formed a pattern in the way we worked. Carol would pose a question which I would answer to the best of my ability. Then she probed deeper, sometimes arguing with my response, yet often agreeing. It made for a lively two to three hours.

"Let me share in your thoughts," I said at last.

She looked up, now making eye contact. "Are there still other areas I haven't developed? Are there other issues still to be resolved in future lives?" She laughed, self-consciously. "I want it all now. Intellectually, I know I'm not perfect, but yet . . . "

"Why don't we see?" I suggested. "Do you want to try another regression?"

She sighed. "Not if it makes me as uncomfortable as Hans's did . . . But I guess I'll never know if I don't chance it. Sure. Let's go ahead."

We discussed focusing on another concern in this session. Carol suggested "weight," as she confided that she had been trying to lose fifteen to twenty pounds for a long time without much success. The induction process was as before . . .

Once again I asked her to look down at her feet and tell me what she saw.

"I'm barefoot and there's dust . . . "

"Dust?" I interrupted, thinking I had misunderstood her.

"Dust," she repeated.

"Now look at your body and tell me what clothes you have on . . . if any."

"It's . . . it's rags," she answered with a surprised lift to her voice. She described her hair as black and long.

"I'm young," she announced. " . . . a young girl about ten."

"Look around you now. Where are you located? What type of buildings? Are you outside . . . or what?"

"I'm outside. On a street. It's dusty."

"Describe to me what you see as you walk along the street," I said.

"I see people . . . carriages . . . it's dirty. There's garbage in the street, horse droppings. Smells." She wrinkled her nose slightly.

"Do you know the name of this town . . . or place?"

"I think it's Birmingham."

I assumed she meant Birmingham, Alabama, but almost as an afterthought, just to be certain, I asked, "Where's Birmingham located?"

"In . . . England."

It only proved you couldn't take anything for granted. "What's the year?"

"Late . . . late 1800s. It's 1890. It's almost the twentieth century."

"Continue to walk down the street," I directed. "When you see a street sign, can you read that to me? Tell me what street it is."

"Man...chester," she said matter-of-factly. "I know that's the street, but I can't read the letters."

"How do you know that's the street?"

"Because people say it is."

"Where do you live?"

"Under a bridge."

"What happened to your parents?"

"My father ran off. Mother's there with the others."

"What others?"

"The other children. I'm almost the oldest," she said proudly.

"So your mother and the other children live under the bridge, too?" I repeated to be sure I had all the facts right.

"We had a house . . . " she said defensively. "I don't remember where. But they put us out."

"Who put you out?"

"The registry. We didn't have any money."

"The registry?" I said. I wasn't familiar with the term.

"The court," she answered patiently as though talking to a child. " . . . the registry from the court."

"What's your name?"

Often, in other lives, Carol had struggled to "hear" her name. This time it came quickly in response to my question. "Anna."

"Anna, what's your last name?"

She shook her head. "I don't know."

I checked my notepad and noticed that she had said she was ten years old. "Do you go to school?" She shook her head. "What do you do during the day?"

"Go to the train station and beg for money."

"Do you make much money?"

"No." She grinned like a little girl. "Take fruit at the green grocers, too. When he's not looking. Play with the others. There's a lot of kids on the street."

I asked her if she were a happy or unhappy girl. She looked surprised, as though she had never considered that thought before. "I guess I'm happy. I don't know."

I wanted to see if the issue of weight, which Carol had wanted to explore, was present in this life. "Look at yourself, Anna. Tell me how you look."

Her eyes fluttered. "Dirty . . . skinny . . . hair's matted. I'm cold. It's getting cold."

Obviously, she didn't want to deal with issues of weight at this point. It was time to have her advance or retreat to a different period in Anna's life. She chose to go ahead by just four years.

"I'm about fourteen . . . and I've got me a job in a big house . . . doing the pots and dishes in the kitchen." She sounded joyful. "They took me in and gave me a uniform to wear and a room to sleep in. There's two other girls. So it's like I got friends. It's nice."

"What are you doing right now? What's making this significant for you?"

I was surprised by her answer. "I have a bed with sheets and a blanket and something to sleep in . . . not my clothes. It's lovely." Later, after this regression, Carol confided that she was almost compulsive about her bedsheets, purchasing the highest thread count possible so they'd be soft and then changing them twice a week.

We tried another period in Anna's life. This time, she went to a later date.

"They want me to go to hospital," she announced abruptly.

"Who's 'they'?"

"Cook and the others. I've been there so long but . . . I'm . . . I'm coughing and they say I'm sick. I don't want to go because nobody gets out of hospital alive. I tell them I'll be all right. I can work." She paused, struck by a violent coughing attack. Concerned, I was about to bring her out of the state when the coughing ceased. She continued. "But they take me in the big carriage to hospital anyway." Her voice grew sad. "I know I won't be seeing them any more."

She told me that she was now thirty. She had worked in the same household all these years. Then she bragged a little.

"Wasn't always in the kitchen, though. They gave me a different uniform 'cause I was cleaning and working upstairs. They were so good to me. There was no reason for me to want to leave. Jobs aren't that easy to come by. Here in hospital I got sheets and a pillow, but it's not the same."

"What's the name of the people who own the house?"

"Martin."

"Is that the last name? First name?"

"Last name. He has a steel mill. Bernard Martin."

"What's the name of the steel mill?"

"'Iron Works' is all I remember. They've been so good."

"Have you married at all?"

Here Anna grew coy. "No. I've had some boyfriends, though, but I've never married."

"Has life been good or bad for you?"

"Good. Had friends there . . . good job."

I tried to focus on the weight issue again. "Eaten well?"

"Yes."

"Have you ever had any problem with your weight?"

"No. I'm healthy." Then she added reluctantly, "Was healthy 'til I started coughing."

So much for trying to "lead" a subject. No matter how hard Carol claimed she wanted to discuss weight, her subconscious mind was having none of it. I could tell she was tiring so I decided to bring her along to the time of Anna's death.

"Tell me what happens next. They take you to the hospital in the carriage now. Go on."

"Take me there. They take away my clothes and give me a gown to put on. It's striped and it's rough. Sister puts me in bed. There's all kinds of people in the room. They're coughing . . . I just feel like it's hard to catch my breath. I don't tell them I've been coughing up blood . . . 'cause I think they'll let me go back. This doctor comes in. He's got a beard and he looks at me. He shakes his head and he goes on to the next one. I'd leave but I don't know where they've put my clothes."

"Do you know the name of the hospital?"

"Prince Edward . . . Prince Edward Hospital."

"Where's it located?"

"In Birmingham."

"What year is it now?"

"1923."

"Could you tell me your last name now?"

"Hodges. Anna May Hodges."

"What happens next?"

"I just . . . stop eating. I'm coughing more. I don't feel so good. Then I'm coughing up blood and they see it. They put a screen around me. I'm not going to go back to the big house." She utters this last so mournfully that I feel sorry for her.

"What's going to happen?"

"I'm going to die in this hospital."

"Anna May, in looking back over your life, is there anything you'd like to tell me about it?"

She shook her head sadly. "I really could have gotten somewhere if I hadn't gotten sick. I really wanted to be somebody . . . my chest hurts," she added, almost childlike.

"Anna, if you're at peace now, you can allow your death to occur . . . tell me when your spirit or soul leaves your body."

"I'm being drawn up . . . like the sky opens up. There's lights and it's . . . so many people."

"How do you feel?"

"Light."

"Is there anybody there that you recognize?"

"I see . . . I see Carol's husband there. I don't think he was with Anna, but he's there and so many friends are there. It's like a shore . . . like the beach and all these people are waving."

"Do they have clothes on or is it just their face? Like you

see Carol's husband . . . is it just his face or is he wearing something?"

She frowned as she studied the scene. "No, he's got . . . like a . . . like a . . . a brown shirt and slacks, but they sort of flow. Everyone is so happy. I feel the . . . the sounds of the surf and the sun. It's just wonderful. Oh, I embrace everything."

She seemed so caught up in this sense of joy that I hated to break in. "What lesson did Anna May need to learn in her lifetime?"

"To make something of herself. She waited too late."

There it was again. The same message she had received—and wanted to reject—from Hans. I knew we would have an interesting discussion after *this* regression.

"How is that applicable to Carol?" I asked. "In her present lifetime?"

"She . . . took a long time to think of herself. Wasted some important early years. Under the bridge too long."

"What was the purpose of Anna May's life?"

"Well, she served the Martins well . . . and was a good worker . . . but she really left no one behind to mourn her. That's sad."

I was about to take her out of the hypnotic state, when a thought occurred to me. "Before you pass back through that yellow door, are there any of the monks or anybody else with you?"

"There was a figure that took me to see the other people . . . it was . . . she was in back of me, but it was a female form and it was brightness, but I don't know . . . it was a female form, but I don't recognize it."

"Is that gone now?"

"Yes," she answered softly. Accordingly, I brought her out. She sat for a few moments, getting back in touch with the present. "So much for discussing my weight problem," she said at last.

"I don't think you were ready. It seems as though there was something else to work through."

"It's Hans again, isn't it?" she questioned, resigned.

"It's Hans," I agreed.

"I'm blocking him out."

"I know," I said. We sat looking at each other.

After a few moments of silent reflection, I began. "Carol, you don't like not getting your way . . . or not accomplishing what you set out to do. In your present body and physical being, it's hard for you to accept the possibility of not having achieved early life goals. Both Hans and Anna May felt that they waited too long for their individual aspirations. This fact hasn't been easily digested as it developed that you also took a long time to think of yourself . . . and that you, too, wasted some important early years."

The reinforcement of still unresolved issues appeared to hit her hard. Slowly, somewhat introspectively, Carol nodded acknowledgment. Her dislike of Hans could be understood, for in Carol's mind this highlighted her perceived failure. In time, Carol would come to terms with her new understanding. She would find relief with the knowledge that this issue would be "settled" in a life still to come.

CAROL

This regression made a deep impression on me, as did the previous one with my nemesis, Hans. Both made me feel uneasy, as though I've left some unfinished business, which, of course, it seems I have. Just mentioning Hans's name conjures up a sense of anxiety. I wonder if I could be regressed to Hans's life again and, if so, what more could I discover.

Anna's life, too, has touched me in this life. I've always been drawn to the Victorian era and, specifically, in England. If questioned before this regression, however, I would have said I must have been "Lady Something or Other" from a posh section of London. How ironic to discover that I was from the lower class and from Birmingham.

Anna's life, as experienced in this regression, was replete with specific details, many of which were verifiable: I learned that Birmingham *is* a "sooty" town, explaining why Anna kept referring to "dust." Also, there *is* a Manchester Street about half a mile from the train station.

I called Birmingham, England, to pin down some additional details. A *King* Edward School does exist in Birmingham, but not a hospital. However, the building *was* used as an infirmary during World War I, around the period that Anna was admitted as a patient.

I also contacted the Historical Department of the Birmingham City Council and learned that there was a Martin & Co. Metal Manufacturing plant at the turn of the century. Could this have been the "iron works" owned by Anna's employer, Bernard Martin?

There were many examples of "spillover" from Anna's life into mine, which is interesting because her life must have been the one just prior to my present one. Anna found it significant to have a bed with sheets. While I think Dr. Klein thought it strange that this was a "significant" event, I didn't. In this life, I have always "had a thing" for sheets and buy the highest thread count so they are soft.

In my childhood I had a recurring dream in which I was in a bed in a long room filled with rows of beds and a hand came down and plucked me upward. I wonder if this was a past-life memory of Anna dying in the hospital ward.

Anna found it sad to have died without leaving anyone behind. Could this be a reason why from childhood on I was always determined to have a large family? Why my favorite books were *Eight Cousins, Five Little Peppers, Little Men,* and *Little Women?*

So much of this regression was extremely vivid. The fact that although I couldn't read the street sign, I knew what it was. The verbiage of "we were put out by the registry from the court" and "I got me a job" seemed so spontaneous, yet it's not the way I usually speak. Also, while replaying the tape, I heard myself cough as I described my illness. My olfactory senses also were sharpened as the odor of the street dust and the horse droppings was extremely intense.

I know I'm resisting the messages being shouted from these two past lives despite Dr. Klein's explanation. Obviously, I also missed the opportunity in *this* life to make the necessary changes. I really feel haunted by this nonfulfillment.

12

WEIGHT LOSS AT LAST

DR. KLEIN

*I*t was four weeks before Carol and I met again. We had planned for a two-week hiatus as we both had professional conferences to attend. I also sensed that Carol needed some time away from this project.

"It's gotten pretty intense," she admitted.

"Too much so?" I asked, with some concern. Although I was anxious to publish our findings, I did not want to do so at any risk to my co-author.

"No . . ." she said hesitantly. Then, more confidently, "No. It's fine. But so much has come out of these past lives. I'm looking forward to getting some distance—both physically and emotionally—so that I can process it all."

The two weeks flew by. I was surprised at how much I was looking forward to getting back to work with Carol. I knew we had an important message to tell and was anxious to compile all of our material in written form.

The day of our next meeting, two hours before our session was scheduled, I received a call from Carol. I knew from her voice that something was troubling her.

"I'm having a bad nosebleed," she said shakily. "I've been referred to an ENT specialist. I'm stopping off there before I come to see you. I may be late."

"Have you had one before?"

"This is the sixth in less than a week," she admitted.

"Are they bad?"

"They've all lasted at least half an hour, some an hour."

She sounded weak and tired. "How long have you had this one?" I asked.

"Two hours."

Something *was* wrong. "Go ahead with your appointment. Call me when you're through. If you don't feel up to getting together, we'll postpone 'til next week."

"No, I'll be fine," she said, none too convincingly.

Almost two hours later, Carol's son appeared in my office. "Mom's downstairs at the doctor's," he said. "She'll have to cancel her appointment with you."

Coincidence? The specialist Carol had been referred to had his office in the same building as mine. I accompanied Carol's son downstairs. She was in one of the examining rooms, leaning in a semireclining position, her nose packed so the bleeding would stop.

"I think it's an arterial bleed," the otolaryngologist informed me. "Too high up to cauterize. She's lost a great deal of blood in the last few days."

He sent Carol home, insisting that she stay there, resting as much as possible for a two-week period. An active person, she fussed, but it was a lukewarm protest without much conviction.

We talked by phone during what she referred to as her "house arrest," but I didn't want to overtax her.

After being released by her physician, Carol resumed the meetings with me. Still anemic, she tired easily so I tried to help her pace herself.

"Let's try another regression," she urged. "How about attempting the 'weight' issue again?"

Reluctantly, I agreed. Her enthusiasm was contagious and I *was* anxious to continue.

"After all this time, what if I can't go into the hypnotic state? What if I've forgotten how?" she asked with a worried tone in her voice.

I couldn't help laughing. "We're back to your original concern." I reminded her that "If you don't . . . "

" . . . you don't," she finished.

"Ready?"

She nodded and before I had gotten too far into the regular induction, Carol was in a very deep trance state.

"What's on your feet?" I asked as usual.

"Sandals . . . brown, with lacings up my legs."

"Look at your body and tell me what kind of clothes, if any, that you have on."

"It's like a . . . white shift . . . "

"And your hair? What color is it?"

"Brown."

"About how old would you say you are right now?"

"Fifties."

"Look about you," I instructed. "What do you see around you? Landscape . . . city . . . whatever."

Her eyes fluttered as she took in the physical scene. "I'm in a . . . inside . . . it's a . . . rich person's house. Lots of gold . . . marble . . . pillars . . . "

"What room are you in now?"

"I . . . think it's a banquet hall or . . . there are many tables with food . . . "

"Why are you in this house?"

Her forehead wrinkled as she concentrated. "I think I work for the . . . I work for the person who lives there. Do something with . . . like an auditor . . . it's a . . . it seems to be . . . Rome . . . people in togas . . . with lots of servants around. I'm not a servant . . . I'm part of the staff." The distinction seemed important to her. "There are guards . . . wearing armor over their chests. They're wearing like skirts with metal boots . . . and they stand guard . . . "

"Could you describe their armor a little more? Take a look . . . see what the details are."

"Curlicues over the breast plate. It fits down over the chest . . . and goes as far as their privates. It's very ornate . . . gold . . . gilded . . . they carry spears, also very ornate. Wavy. With designs like . . . don't think it's . . . like bird wings . . . "

"Are there any crests on this armor? Or the spears? Anybody's name?"

Carol shook her head.

"Are there any crests in the house? Who is the master . . . the owner of the house?"

"Lucius . . . Lucius Marius . . . "

"What is your name?"

"Cadreci," she answered without hesitation. "I keep his books."

"Cadreci, what year is this?"

"I don't know."

"Could you tell me what land this is?"

"It's Rome. He is . . . grains, wheat, I think. He's not a farmer. He's . . . he is . . . like the middle man."

"Cadreci, do you live at the house?"

"I have apartments in the house." She answered the question proudly, as though actually living in the house was some kind of a "perk."

"Where do you keep the books?"

"There's a room on the main floor."

"Could you go to that room to look at your books? Go ahead to that room. Open up your books. Tell me what you see. Read it to me."

"There are columns . . . "

"Do they have a date? What's the date at the top of the page?"

"Five-twenty," she said matter-of-factly. "There's listings of . . . slaves . . . of household objects . . . of carriages . . . of wine . . . " Her voice faded away as though she was skimming the rest of the contents.

"How long have you been working for Lucius?"

"I worked for his father before. Then, when the father died, I began to work for Lucius. He's young. He trusts me . . . which he probably shouldn't."

"Why's that?"

"Because I manipulate the books for my own advantage. I say I do it because his father cheated me . . . but the boy has faith in me. It's really not fair. But I feel it's my . . . it's owed me," she said defensively.

"Owed you?" Obviously, there was more to Cadreci's story. I wanted to learn what it was. I suggested we go to a significant time in Cadreci's life. He went back in time.

"I'm a young man . . . I have a good mind and a good future."

"How old are you?"

"Early twenties. Twenty-two, I think."

"And your name?"

"Cadreci. I want to be a warrior . . . but I have . . . I have a weakness so instead they have me do things of the mind rather than of the body. All my friends are drilling and becoming part of the guard."

"What is your weakness?"

Carol's eyes fluttered. "I can't see what it is . . . I look all right. I . . . I don't know what it is. It's . . . I can't see what it is," she said helplessly.

"That's all right, Cadreci. What's significant about this time? You're in your early twenties. You want to be a warrior, but you're not. Is there anything else that happens?"

"I . . . I'm disappointed . . . I'm asked to come to this merchant's house to learn to keep his books."

"Do you go?"

A disgusted look crossed her face. "Yes, I do. He . . . he takes to me. He wants me as a lover. I'm repelled by it. He's a well-known merchant. He has a wife. I didn't know this side of him." She lowers her voice. "He tells me if I do as he asks, he'll take care of me. Oh . . . I want . . . I want the position . . . I want the stature . . . I want the power that I think he'll give me so I give in to him. He lied. He sickens me."

"How did he lie?" I asked.

"He promised that he would take care of me after his death and he doesn't. He leaves it to his son. So it's owed me."

"What is his name?"

"The son's name is Lucius Marius. He trusts me because his father said I was a good man. So I take what's due me. Right from under his son's eyes." She laughs as though enjoying a good joke. "He doesn't even know."

"I see. So you worked for the father first and then the son. It was the father who . . . took you sexually and didn't give you anything."

"Yes," she sighed. "He made me ashamed. I never . . . I never was fit for a woman after that. It was his fault. I hated him. He was . . . he broke his promise to me."

"What did you do? Anything?"

"I eat."

There it was. At last, the weight issue was being confronted. "Why is that?"

"It's all he's left for me," she said sadly.

"What do you mean?"

"I can't know a woman . . . I can't stand to touch a man. He's made me a eunuch . . . without the surgery."

I felt as though we had touched on an important concern. I wanted to try to connect some of the loose ends. "Cadreci, what we're going to do is try to go back to a period in your life . . . you mentioned that you had a weakness . . . to see if we can find out what this weakness was. Maybe it will be a time in your life when you understood that. When I count to three, you'll go there. One . . . two . . . three . . . What's happening, Cadreci?"

Again, her eyes fluttered as though she were watching a movie screen. "I . . . I'm five . . . or maybe six. I'm running and playing on some rocks. I fall. Oh, I . . . I've bruised my knee. I go home to my mother. She puts hot oil towels on my knee. But in the morning it's . . . it's swollen, stiff, and sore. I . . . I'm a bleeder. I . . . when I hurt myself, I bleed. My knees swell, my leg . . . I can't play like the other boys. She wants to keep me home like a girl and I won't let that happen. But I can't keep up with them . . . so I study . . . I compensate . . . I limp from bleeding. My knees . . . they stay swollen a lot . . . The oil doesn't help."

"What stops the bleeding?"

"I rest . . . it eventually absorbs, but . . . when there's a cut on my hand, it . . . we put pressure and it stops . . . but it's the other . . . other bleeds that hurt so."

"Which other bleeding?"

"The ones that don't come from a cut. The inside bleeds."

"What other bleeds do you have?"

"Sometimes my ears . . . sometimes my nose . . . I bruise . . . It makes me weak."

"How do you get your strength back?"

"My mother feeds me nectar . . . a drink . . . a sweet drink. When the bleeding goes away, then I'm all right."

A lot had evolved. Sensing that Carol was tired, I decided to move along to the end of this life.

Her head turned from side to side. She obviously was in discomfort. "I'm bleeding from everywhere . . . I'm lying on a . . . like a lounge. It's covered with red."

"How old are you?"

"Fifty-five."

"Are you by yourself?"

"No . . . Lucius is here . . . oh, he's stroking me." She laughed. "He doesn't know it's like his father used to. He doesn't want me to leave him. I think I had too much wine or something and I've just . . . the life is draining out of me. I want to tell Lucius what his father did to me . . . but I keep quiet. I haven't the strength." She paused, her eyes filling with tears. "I . . . cared for the boy. I . . . I hated his father, but I loved the boy."

She continued to toss fitfully, her head moving from side to side, her face contorting in pain. Quickly, I encouraged her to go to the time when the spirit left Cadreci's body.

In a few seconds, her body relaxed. "I'm above him now," she whispered.

"Have you arrived at the in-between state? The plane state?"

"Yes."

I asked her what Cadreci had learned in his lifetime.

"That love is the answer. That love overrules revenge. There's beauty in that. Cadreci found beauty in love, but he didn't recognize it."

"What did he find beauty in?"

"The boy. Lucius. Cadreci cared for him. Cheated him . . . but he loved him."

"Are there any other lessons?"

She almost spat out the answer. "He might have lived longer if he hadn't gotten so fat."

"Why is that?"

"Because he might not have bled . . . if he had stayed slim he might have been able to keep his body functioning longer. He had a weakness and he allowed it to possess him, out of anger and bitterness."

"How does this apply to Carol in her present life?"

"She must take better care of the body she has if she wants to stay with those she loves."

"What was the purpose of Cadreci's life?"

She sounded far away. "He had to learn that love was

more powerful than hate . . . that was why he was there. That was why he had to learn what he did."

"Is there anybody in Cadreci's life that reminded you of somebody in Carol's present life?"

To my surprise, Carol burst into heaving sobs. "Lucius was . . . her brother." Interestingly, and understandably, I knew from our previous conversations that Carol had been extremely close to a younger brother who had died suddenly.

It was obvious that this extraordinary past-life experience had exacted an enormous toll on Carol, especially in her anemic condition. I didn't want to drain her energies any longer so I moved her back into the garden. Here I instructed her to rest comfortably and peacefully for a few minutes, giving suggestions that enabled her to relax. I added, "You'll be able to remember all that has transpired, profiting from what you've discovered."

After her eyes opened, Carol sat for a full minute in silence. I respected her need for reflection and waited. At last she looked at me, biting her lip.

"Wow," was all she said.

"There's a lot to deal with," I acknowledged.

She nodded. "I'm beat. Funny . . . I had felt great apprehension coming into the session today. I knew I wanted to use 'weight' for an issue, but felt a lot of anxiety as to what, if anything, would come out."

I remained silent, sensing that she needed time to collect and express her thoughts. They came tumbling out.

"I had the overwhelming sensation that 'nothing would happen,'" she confessed. "Yet, as soon as I began to visualize the staircase, I felt myself going into the darkness that I have begun to associate with the hypnotic state."

"You were in a very deep state this time," I added.

She nodded. "I sensed that. As soon as I entered into my past life as Cadreci and saw myself as obese and somewhat balding, I felt a distinct uneasiness . . . sort of a foreboding of sordidness." She hesitated, then accused, "You didn't ask me what I looked like. I would have said that I was fat and disgusting. My legs were thick and ugly."

"I purposely didn't," I told her. "I didn't want to focus on your appearance, didn't want to lead you in any way."

"Oh." Then . . . "Part of me wanted to censor my descriptions to you, to hide what I was seeing and experiencing. I didn't, though. I guess that's because I feel a flow of trust between us." She looked directly at me, as though seeking verification. I nodded.

Carol paused, her eyes filling with tears. She swallowed hard. "The warmth of love I discovered for Lucius shortly before my death surprised me. I didn't want to leave him—yet, I was suddenly and completely aware of the knowledge that by experiencing such love, I had learned what I had come to that life for . . . and that it was time to move on." Her voice broke. "Lucius' eyes were those of my brother. I have absolutely no doubt of that."

I gave her time to regain her composure before continuing to pursue another area. "How did you feel about the homosexuality?" I asked.

"I was embarrassed to tell you," she admitted. "It was unpleasant, not enjoyable in any way. It made me feel . . . " she stopped mid-sentence, her eyes widening as she discovered new meaning in what she had experienced.

"What are you thinking?"

"It's just that . . . that what I felt most was that I was being used. Obviously, I had given silent consent—I would permit being used in return for his giving me approval and position—but the fact remains: he manipulated me and I wasn't assertive enough to say no. It's back to that old problem I've struggled with so often—in this life and others—not being assertive, not standing up for me. I've let others take advantage of me for their own benefit. In Cadreci's life, it was being exploited sexually. In others, I'm maneuvered in different ways. But it all comes down to lack of assertiveness." She leaned back in her chair, spent by her outburst.

"Anything else?" I asked, not wanting to break her train of thought.

"Just the power of the message, that I need to take care of this body. I've known I needed to drop about twenty pounds. This made it very graphic. I guess the nosebleeds—which the doctor doesn't really know *why* they occurred—were a warning."

"It's interesting," I added. "Here you are fifty-five years old—the same age as Cadreci when he died. Also, rather recently, there has been a further increase in your weight. You mentioned a warning and I concur. Cadreci died by bleeding to death. Obviously, his poor health was heightened by his excessive weight. Remember the lesson that was relayed to you—'She must take better care of the body she has if she wants to stay with those she loves.' Cadreci felt he had nothing left in life. He was frustrated and so he ate, that being his only pleasure. You needn't do the same.

"Now we can understand the origins of your inappropriate eating patterns. You, like Cadreci, find pleasure in eating as a method of dealing with frustration. Of course, you have other outlets for pleasure that he didn't—but you still handle stress in much the same way—with food. You need to develop healthier methods for coping."

Carol continued to quietly digest what was being said, so I continued. "Many lessons could be learned from Cadreci. Power and wealth aren't worth the sacrifice of one's principles—for, if this route is chosen, eventually self-destruction will occur. If misled by others, revenge is not an answer, because eventually you become deceitful. At that point, only guilt, not satisfaction, will arise. Love should override anger as this emotion can be more powerful than hate."

CAROL

I'm still numb by the impact of this regression. I can't help being amazed at the strange voyage of self-discovery I have embarked upon. A message from the past leads me into taking long-awaited action—losing weight. What resolve and wishes in my present life couldn't do, Cadreci's death in a previous life has achieved.

I have cut my fat grams considerably since this regression. It seems to be intuitive, not studied. Like two similar magnetic poles repelling each other, I turn away from some of my former temptations—ice cream, pie, and beef. Never a heavy drinker, I also seem to have lost my taste for alcohol. I look forward to exercising and, as soon as the ENT specialist approves, will return to watching the morning news from my moving treadmill.

It's six weeks later. I have had no further nosebleeds and thus far have lost ten pounds rather effortlessly. I feel great and am becoming most comfortable with further asserting myself. Experiencing Cadreci's death has certainly played an enormous role in the living of my life.

13

ASKING FOR HELP

DR. KLEIN

"*I* want to do another regression, but this time, try to pin me down on details," Carol announced when we got together again. "Let's try to get some hard facts."

"Whom do you need to convince?"

She grinned. "I guess myself to some slight degree. But I'd like to prove to naysayers that these experiences aren't just an active imagination."

"Those with closed minds are difficult to sway," I warned her. "Galileo was just recently acknowledged to be correct—three hundred and fifty years after being censored by the Inquisition."

"I've got plenty of time," she assured me. "If not in this lifetime, then another."

As before, we set up the tape recorder so we'd have a permanent record of what transpired. She leaned back in the chair as she had done so many times previously. Before I could instruct her to take deep breaths, her eyes drooped and closed. Soon, I knew, we would be able to conduct the induction in just a few words.

"You've stepped through the door?" I asked. She nodded.

"Look down at your feet. Tell me what you see."

"Boots," she replied. "Brown cowboy boots." Her voice reflected a sense of surprise as it often did at what she was wearing.

"Now look at your body. Tell me what you have on."

"Tight pants, flannel shirt."

"Anything else?"

"No."

"Can you tell me what your name is?"

"Bob," she said simply.

"Bob, what is your last name?"

"Davidson."

I asked her to look around and tell me what she saw.

Her closed eyes surveyed the surroundings. "Open space. Grass."

"Is it mountains or flat prairie?"

"Hills in the background. But there's lots of open space."

"About how old are you now, Bob?"

"Thirty-four."

"Do you live in this area?"

"Yeah."

Bob obviously was a laconic cowboy. I was going to have to press to get information. I asked him to return to the place he called home. "Can you tell me what you're looking at? What do you see?"

"There's a cabin . . . wood cabin . . . got a wooden table . . . chair . . . all made out of wood . . . "

"Do you live by yourself or with someone?"

"By myself."

"Is that because you've never married or have you married . . . "

"Nope. Never married."

It was like talking to Gary Cooper. I pushed on. "Is this cabin out in the wilderness?"

"Yeah."

"Do you like it there?"

"Love it."

"What type of work do you do? Or activity?"

"Odd jobs. Cowboy . . . different things."

"Are you a cowboy?"

"Well, I work with cattle. Mend fences. I'm good with my hands."

Mindful of Carol's request to get as specific as possible, I asked, "Whom do you work for?"

"A rancher."

"What is his name?"

"I don't know."

"What's the name of the ranch?"

"Double R Bar."

"Double Bar R?"

"Double R Bar. Brand's two R's and then a long flat piece."

"Do you like working for this rancher?" I was well aware I was asking yes and no questions and that it was unlikely that Bob would expand on his answers. Still, I thought it important to get a sense of this cowboy and his personality.

"Yeah," was the reply.

"Can you tell me the year?"

"1800s."

"Where are you? What state is this?"

"It's Wyoming, but I don't think it is a state."

I suggested to Bob that he move to a significant time in his life. He moved to near the end of it.

"I'm sitting on a chair. I'm old and tired. I'm not working. Someone's taking care of me."

"Do you know who this is . . . taking care of you?"

"It's a woman, but I'm not married to her. I'm coughing a lot. She puts a rug around my shoulders. The sun's going down. My legs feel cold."

"What's going to happen?"

"I'm going to sleep."

"Are you going to die?"

"Yeah."

I wasn't ready for that to happen. We needed to explore more of this particular life. "Before you do that," I said, "I'd like you to turn to another part of your life, an earlier part when something happens, something important to you." I counted to three. The transformation on Carol's face was amazing. Where, just seconds before, she had looked wrinkled with sunken eyes, she now looked youthful and healthy, her skin taut. Even her speech pattern had changed.

"I'm eighteen," she said in a strong voice. "My parents have brought me west, brought me to school. I've never been to school. I don't think I can read. I'm too big for school. It's all little kids. I can't read and I feel stupid. The teacher's nice. She's younger than I am, but she's nice . . . When the kids go out to play, she helps me."

"What town is this?"

"Wind Song. It's not much of a town."

"Is it in Wyoming?"

"I think it's Wyoming . . . It's just a street or so."

"What's in this town?"

Again, Carol's eyes flickered as though she were viewing a movie or television show. "A hotel . . . "

"What's it called?"

"Starts with an 'L.'"

"Walk down the street. You can see it."

"Church is at one end . . . far end. I'm not much for churches. There's a blacksmith . . . candlemaker . . . store to get food . . . clothes. Bar across the street."

"What's the name of the bar?"

"Blackie's. He's the blacksmith, too. There's a bank."

"What's the name of that?"

"Gold . . . Golden . . . something. I can't read it. Hard to read."

"Are you familiar with money? Do you handle money?"

"Don't have much."

"Do you have any in your pocket?"

"Yeah."

"Take it out and look at it. Tell me what you see. Coins? Certificates?"

"Coins. Picture of a man on one. Writing on the little one."

"Do you know what it says?"

"No. The writing's all squinchy. There's numbers on it."

"What do the numbers say?"

"There's a six in it."

"Any pictures on that coin?"

"Picture of a lady. Looks like a lady."

"Is it just a face?"

"No. It's a funny lady. It's not really a lady. It's a fancy lady. I don't have much. I trade a lot."

"On the other side of the coin with the picture of the funny lady on it," I persisted, "is there anything on it?"

"There's a star."

"On the other side of the coin? A star? Big star?"

"No."

"Small star?"

She nodded. "It's a small star."

"What color is this coin . . . what metal?"

"One's gray and one's gold. The big one's gold. I think it's a five-dollar coin."

"Is that the one with the picture of the man?"

"Yeah. Little one's silver."

"What makes the picture . . . on the small one . . . what makes the lady funny?"

"She's thin. She's . . . I don't think she has feet. She has wings."

" . . . And the gold coin . . . the five-dollar gold coin. It's a picture of a man?"

"Yes."

I knew I was spending a great deal of time questioning Bob about the money. But here was a specific that we could check. It was the type of "fact" that Carol had requested. "Is there writing?"

She nodded. "There's writing on one side and he's on the other side. I don't know who it is."

"What is the man doing? Is he just a face?"

"Just a face. He's just looking. Got a mustache."

I could tell that Bob's attention span was wandering, so I tried another area. "You attend school? Did you stay in school?"

"No. I got a job working on the fences. I can read a little."

"Whom do you work for?" I had asked this question before, but Bob had been unable to come up with the name.

"A big rancher."

"What's his name?"

"Dean or Don . . . we call him Mister Fields."

"What's the name of his ranch again?"

"Double R Bar."

"Anything else you want to tell me about this time?"

"It's a happy time. I get to ride anywhere I want, feel wind in my face. I like the outdoors. That's what I didn't like about school. Indoors. My parents died, but it doesn't change much. I still work."

I asked Bob to return to what he had experienced before, himself as an old man, sitting in the chair. As I watched, Carol's jaw grew slack, her eyes sank back into her head, and her body shrank down into the cushions of the chair. "It's just before your death," I said softly. "Are there any experiences or anything Bob learned that you want to share before you pass away?"

"I'm lonely. It's lonely. I'm going to sleep . . . he just falls asleep. Then . . . the clouds open up. Now I'm above Bob."

"Where are you now?"

"Flying . . . over the fields."

"While you're in this in-between state . . . can you tell me what lessons Bob learned in his lifetime?"

"Be self-reliant. Do a good job. Be good at what he does."

"How are these lessons applicable to the lifetime of Carol?"

"To be good at what she's good at . . . there's a lot . . . she's lopsided, too. She does what she's good at but . . . but I guess misses out on other things."

"What was the purpose of Bob's life?"

"To achieve . . . to develop . . . couldn't read, but was looked up to. Did a full day's work."

I could see that this life had been tiring to Carol. Her voice faltered, so I had her return to the comfort and safety of the garden and brought her out of the hypnotic state.

"What a sad end," she remarked shortly after her eyes opened.

"Why sad?" I responded, somewhat surprised by her reaction. "Here's a life that you worked hard in and did the best you could with what you had. A very honorable life. Yes, you were somewhat limited with your skills, but that didn't stop you. You were self-reliant and achieved within your boundaries; you lived up to your capabilities.

"Carol, this is what you need to do: Try to aspire to heights that embrace your potential. Realize that everyone has limitations in some areas; it's okay to ask for help when needed, just as Bob required assistance from the schoolteacher. Utilize your abilities to your fullest. Do the best you can; as a result, peace and a feeling of fulfillment should naturally follow."

14

DISCOVERIES

CAROL

*T*he regression to my life as a cowboy, Bob, once again, seemed akin to watching a movie unfold before my eyes. Dr. Klein and I achieved our goal in that this particular regression contained many details that I have attempted to verify. It also included information that I am sure *I* did not know before, but that was readily available and well known to Bob.

He, Bob, that is, *was* accurate in saying that Wyoming had not as yet become a state, but was rather a territory. It didn't achieve statehood until 1890. He described his surroundings as encompassing a great deal of open space with mountains in the background. Indeed, Wyoming does have that type of landscape, especially in the eastern part of the state. Actually, the word *Wyoming* is an Indian word meaning "upon the great plain." The area he described was and still is a good area for grazing sheep and cattle, which would substantiate his claim of working with cattle and mending fences.

The one-room school Bob described was typical for the period in which he mentioned being taken to class at age eighteen. High school for older students didn't exist in Wyoming until 1875.

Bob described the name of his town as Wind Song. Although today there seems to be no town by that name, there could have been one a hundred years ago, especially as Wyoming does have a Wind River, Wind River Canyon, Wind River Indian Reservation, and Wind River Mountains. But the actual name of Wind Song does not appear on any of the older maps I've studied.

While experiencing Bob's life, I felt my cheeks flush as though being sunburned. When approaching death, I was well aware that my heart was pounding. Dr. Klein reported that, just at my death, I grimaced as though suffering pain. Although these are subjective documentations, they, when combined with more objective data, make for compelling evidence.

For example, further research revealed to me that during Bob's lifetime there *was* a small silver coin—a three-cent piece with a five-pointed star on one side and a liberty head on the back—just as Bob had described as "a funny lady." I have never been "into coins" and to my knowledge have never seen these coins pictured in any book. There also actually was in existence then a five-dollar gold piece with a liberty head on one side and an eagle holding arrows on the back.

There have been many additional details that I have been able to verify from these past lives, facts that I could never had known beforehand. I recall, for instance, that in Anna's life she had worked for a family named "Martin" and that the husband had owned a steel mill with "Iron Works" in the name. I then discovered that there indeed had been the Martin & Co. Metal Manufacturing plant in Birmingham, England, at the turn of the century and that there actually was a Manchester Street not far from the railway station in Birmingham, just as Anna had described. My initial description of Anna's feet were not just that she was barefoot, but also that her feet were dusty. I had never added such graphic material before in any of my previous lives. This detail is important, as my later research revealed that Birmingham was indeed a "sooty" town.

The stone houses built into the walls described during Gerta's life in ancient Egypt also actually existed, according to numerous historical sources.

Arad, the sixteenth-century hunter, described his catch matter-of-factly as "grouse," a game bird with which I am not familiar, but which actually was killed for food during that period. If asked prior to experiencing Arad's life to name a number of birds killed for food or sport, I never would have come up with "grouse."

Even Aganda's description of making clay pots matches that detailed in the *World Book Encyclopedia,* down to first wetting one's hands, shaping the spout with fingers, and letting the finished product dry for two days.

All the details of my birth, including the fact that my father was in the delivery room, unusual for the time, have been verified.

Finally, the coin with the hole in it that Hans described in the fish shop actually existed in the 1600s, the time period in which Hans lived. And, although my conscious mind told me it didn't make sense for a fisherman to be wearing wooden shoes because they could get wet, my foray into numerous history books said otherwise; fishermen did wear wooden shoes *because* they were impervious to the effects of the sea.

Doubters, of course, will say that each of these specific points could have come from a long-forgotten movie or television show or perhaps a novel read in my youth, a theory dubbed "cryptomnesia." The irony is that in order to prove to these folks that the past-life experiences are "real," one must be able to point to factual data that exist. When you use that evidence for proof, however, they then argue that because the documentation exists you must have known about it before describing such information under hypnosis.

I've concluded that it really isn't necessary or even important to convince skeptics. They'll eventually come along. After all, even Galileo's oppressors did, despite it taking them over three centuries. The ever-increasing numbers who believe it is possible to access one's past lives are growing, and therapists such as Dr. Klein, Dr. Brian Weiss, and others are leading the way. For whatever reasons, many of us are encouraged to continue searching, talking about it to others, and keeping an open mind.

After all, as Dr. Klein pointed out in our first meeting, the goal of all this is help people understand and work out their problems as quickly as possible so that they can go on with happy and productive lives. It isn't necessary to believe in past lives to achieve this, although I personally believe that after experiencing a few past lives, they will believe.

15

REFLECTIONS AT MIDPOINT

CAROL

*B*efore taking a break from our project, Dr. Klein asked me to set down my thoughts concerning past-life therapy and all that has occurred over this nine-month period.

Strange—this initial part of the project running just nine months—not eight or ten, but nine, the normal gestation period for human fetal development. Through past-life regression I've "given birth" to eleven lives during this period. Some of them have been most difficult deliveries, too.

When I think back to when it all began in April of '92, my mind explodes with questions: What was I like before experiencing past-life therapy? Have I changed? If so, how? Did I

anticipate that I would be deeply affected or did I just agree
to meet because I thought it might prove to be an interesting creative assignment? Given what I know now, would I
still have acquiesced to become a subject?

My thoughts whirl like wind in a summer storm. Dr. Klein
is interested in knowing my feelings on the subject, and my
thoughts as well. I'll try to record them objectively, although
my emotions are bubbling to the surface.

To be honest (and possibly cruelly blunt), I first agreed to
meet with Dr. Klein solely out of curiosity. The subject
piqued my interest and offered me the opportunity to understand the phenomenon of past-lives recall from a respected psychiatrist's viewpoint. I think any reporter worth
his or her salt would have probably done the same. I expected only to interview him and then possibly end up with
good material for an article or two. Selfish motive? Sure. But
it was a fair trade. After all, *his* motive, also stated openly,
was that he wanted information on how to write a book
about the work he was doing. I was inquisitive. There was
no subterfuge on either of our parts.

What happened at that initial meeting and why I stepped
through the looking glass, like Lewis Carroll's Alice, I can
only attribute to the fact that the time must have been right
for me to learn about and experience my past lives. I felt
comfortable with Dr. Klein. No, it was more than that. I felt
safe with him. His enthusiasm was contagious, of course,
but I've been in groups with zealous bungie jumpers and
sky divers, yet have never felt drawn to experiment with either of these so-called fun sports.

I agreed to "have a go," as my English friends would say,
with past-life regression purely out of free will and because
I must have felt a deeper need to do so. I hungered to know
who I had been and why I react as I do and did.

That urge is not unique with me. I think this craving exists in many others as well. There *are* more believers in the
Western world today than ever before. They may not all be

building clay mountains like the character in the movie *Close Encounters of the Third Kind*, who senses something is real although he can't see or touch it, but they—we—are there. The mass media reflects this restlessness as well, this anticipation of knowledge not as yet revealed to us. Think about the popularity of TV shows such as "Quantum Leap" and movies like *ET* and *Ghost*. Oh yes, those of you who believe even without scientific evidence: you are not alone in your thinking.

Have I changed because of my "close encounters" with past lives and what they revealed to me? Absolutely, with no qualifiers. I am transformed, filled with a sense of mission, wanting to share what I have learned.

I feel that my search has helped me to become much more open—to others as well as to myself, welcoming new ideas, new traditions and thoughts. I am far more accepting of "what ifs . . . " without being judgmental and now often find myself saying, "Why not? It *could* be."

In some ways, I sense a new closeness to people—friends, acquaintances, and strangers alike—which seems to be mutual, as others have begun to seek me out to share confidences with me, personal stories as well as tales of unexpected happenings.

In some ways, this all is like becoming a trusting child again, letting my imagination run free without censorship; in other ways, it is a newly discovered maturity, learning that I can now protect myself, my time, and my privacy; that Shakespeare was right when he said we first must be true to ourselves. I now comprehend that I can share my thoughts with others without feeling guilty for not accepting *their* words as right and mine as wrong. In truth, we both can be a little right—or, yes, even a little wrong. More important, I've learned that rather than being either right or wrong, there is a vast, exciting, and challenging area of gray.

The past-life therapy *has* been effective in creating profound changes in my life. While fully aware that it is I who has consciously made these adaptations in my reactions to others, I firmly believe that the seed for this knowledge came from my subconscious while experiencing past lives. As Alice in Wonderland said, "Curiouser and curiouser."

DR. KLEIN

Some might wonder at my decision to take a recess at this point in our collaboration. Why not continue until the end? I had been working with Carol for over a year and helped her to resolve many of her issues. I thought it best to take a break because I sensed that she was tiring—not of our project, but rather from the emotional weight of it all. She once described the regressions as "feeling as though I have some rare blood type and I'm here almost weekly to offer up donations. It's not that I don't want to give; I just sometimes feel a little weak afterward."

We had been working almost steadily and I knew she had acquired a great deal of new information. Carol needed time to process and assimilate what we had learned and accomplished. I knew that after a vacation from our project she would come back refreshed and eager to work once again.

We set no specific date at which to get together again. I said that I would call her when it was time, and she readily agreed.

16

Dealing with Death

DR. KLEIN

Although I had deemed it important for us to take a break from our collaboration, I was surprised to find that I missed our sessions. It was like setting aside a novel in which you had been deeply engrossed.

I turned my attention totally back to my practice and with joy continued to see more and more individuals who desired to participate in this type of therapy. Much to my delight, I could see that a change was occurring as to how people perceived themselves and their beliefs.

With vigor I followed up on this "new energy." To satisfy the feeling of a need to reach an even larger audience, I developed a seminar to explain the purpose and techniques of past-life therapy. I thoroughly enjoyed speaking to the general public. To my pleasure, I was usually well received, although a few similar questions kept cropping up which still indicated a great amount of skepticism on the part of some. But this was all right. In fact, I found myself enjoying a lively debate at times.

Soon, however, I began to wonder how a medical institution might perceive me and my work. Thus, although having some initial trepidation, I inquired about speaking at two local hospitals. I need not have been concerned. Within several days, approval arrived, along with specific time and space.

The reinforcement and acceptance I received from my talks was overwhelmingly positive. It felt great. Gradually, as the months rolled along and I experienced additional successes, I sensed that it was time to return to my original plan: writing a book about the healing possibilities of past lives. With my mind focused and feeling that Carol might once again be ready to proceed, I gave her a call.

CAROL

I received a call today from Dr. Klein, although it's been over a year since we last worked together. He has the uncanny knack of knowing exactly when I've just completed an assignment and am temporarily "between projects." I was pleased to hear from him as I had felt a distinct lack of closure with what we had begun.

He suggested that we get together to do a few more past-life regressions and to complete our book at last. Since I originally "interviewed" him and ended up a subject, he has treated many others with past-life therapy. Some of his patients now come from different areas of the country as well as outside of the United States.

At first, I was somewhat reluctant—to attempt to do more past lives. I certainly was not unwilling to finish the book with him. I looked forward to doing so.

My hesitation with regression, as before, is that I'm concerned whether or not it will "work" (that is, that I won't be able to go into the hypnotic state). I'm afraid of failing—that I'll lack the ability to focus. I also admit to feeling some anxiety as to what I will experience if it does work.

He has great tenacity, however. Finally I agreed to come again to his office. My curiosity always tends to get the better of me.

But I could not have arranged a less opportune time for me to meet with Dr. Klein if I had tried. There presently were a number of personal problems in my life. Also, my close friend had just died and I missed her terribly. In addition, I had just completed two major writing projects and was physically and emotionally drained. Nevertheless, I kept our appointment.

We chatted for at least an hour about a number of subjects, including the stress I obviously was feeling. I've never been good at hiding my emotions and certainly wasn't able to conceal them from someone who specializes in such problems. Dr. Klein listened with concern and offered some hints that I sensed would be quite helpful in reducing some of the pressures I was experiencing. He carefully avoided mentioning the past-life project. Finally, he smiled. "Well?"

I nodded. "I'm willing to try again," I said, "but it hasn't been a good few weeks. I can't promise anything."

"You don't have to," he reassured me.

I settled into the comfortable leather chair he had added since my last visit, leaned back, and put my feet on the foot stool. I might just fall asleep, I thought. Dr. Klein busied himself with the tape recorder. The taping system was a much more sophisticated setup than when we had first begun. It now had two microphone leads, one that clipped to my jacket and one to his in order that both voices could clearly be picked up. He dimmed the lights and sat down opposite me. I felt relaxed, as though soaking in a warm tub. Without urging, I closed my eyes. My lids felt heavy and I sensed a floating sensation even before he began the now familiar trance induction.

DR. KLEIN

At first Carol experienced resistance. Although visualizing the garden, she was unable to proceed any further. She seemed comfortable and relaxed, but could not find a door that would lead her to another past life. Thus, I used a method previously successful with her. She, at my suggestion, visualized herself in an elevator. I asked her to choose a floor, and she pushed a button marked "eight." Upon arrival, the elevator opened and she stepped out.

"Look down at your feet and tell me what you see," I said, wanting to give her the chance to ground herself. There was a pause before she answered.

"I don't see anything."

"That's okay. You'll be fine. Just walk in the direction . . . whatever direction you choose. What do you feel under your feet as you walk?" I waited for her to answer.

"I don't feel anything," she said with frustration. "I see clouds. I feel like . . . like I'm nowhere . . . "

I sensed a tone of panic in her voice and wanted to calm and reassure her. "Are you in the in-between state? You've been there before . . . "

There was a pause, as though that thought was being considered. "But I don't feel at peace. I feel fear."

"You feel fear?" I questioned.

"I feel afraid."

"Tell me, what are you fearful of?"

"I don't know," she answered, sounding confused as though she wasn't quite sure what was happening.

"You'll be able to identify where you are in a while. Just continue walking and describe to me how you feel."

"Alone . . . confused," she answered in a childlike voice.

"It's as though I just see clouds. It's not a peaceful feeling. It's as though . . . I may be in the wrong spot."

She spoke so softly I had difficulty in understanding her. "I'm sorry. You were in the what?"

"I think I'm in the wrong place," she said flatly.

"What do you mean?"

"I don't know why I'm here."

"That's fine. You're doing just fine," I said reassuringly. "We'll try to find out where you were after . . . but first, let's describe your body. Feel your hands and tell me what you feel. Are there any rings on your hands or can you feel any clothing on your arms?"

"No. I . . . it's nothing. I sort of feel like I'm not there. I don't feel me. I don't feel anything solid."

"Maybe you're just in the process of traveling to the in-between state. Let your soul go ahead. Tell me where it is."

"I feel as though I'm soaring."

"When you get to the in-between state, when you do feel that peace, tell me." At this moment, the telephone in my office rang. Carol jerked slightly and frowned, although she kept her eyes closed. I spoke softly into the phone and told my secretary to hold future calls. Carol shook her head. "What's happening?" I asked her.

"I felt as though I had lost the markers. I didn't know where to go." She sighed, as though disappointed.

Obviously, she had been roused from the alpha state by the sound of the telephone. I wanted to return her to it quickly. "Okay, let me help you. What we are going to do is to return to whatever body you just came from. You'll go back to that body. It will be before the death experience, before that body died. We'll be able to retrace . . . go back through . . . what had occurred. So I'm going to count to three. Let's reverse the process and go back to the body that you just came from . . . one . . . two . . . three. What's happening now? Describe to me where you're at." This process was done to help her regain her focused concentration.

"There is a pile of bodies piled high. But I don't know where I am."

"That's all right. Describe to me what you see."

She spoke quickly. "I see desert. I see sand. Men. There . . . bodies are being burned. It's a big stack of . . . the bodies are white. I don't . . . " Her voice trailed off.

"Are you watching this? Are you a guard or are you a person, a part of the people who are . . . whoever this is happening to?"

"I feel as though I'm in the pile of bodies. But if I'm dead, why do I . . . am I watching it?"

Carol appeared to be somewhat threatened by what she was witnessing. At times, I sensed that she wanted to come away from this past-life experience as the depth of the hypnotic state was not consistent. Although I wanted to keep her in the alpha state, I was prepared to "take her out" if she seemed too intimidated or uncomfortable. Therefore, I continued to try to help her remain concentrated. "Are you hovering over it or are you in among the bodies? Okay . . . what we'll do is what we did when you went back into the body. When I count to three, you'll go to a time before you saw that pile of bodies. Go to an earlier age." I counted to three. "What's happening? Where are you?"

"I still seem to be in the desert. I'm a little boy."

"Okay. Do you live in the desert? Is that it?"

"Yes, I must. But I'm . . . I . . . I'm lost here, too. I don't seem to belong to anybody." She sounded bewildered.

"What happened to your mother and father?"

"I don't know."

"About how old are you right now?"

She answered immediately and decisively, "Three."

"What do they call you?"

"I don't know. I feel very anxious."

"Is something going to happen to you? Are you running from someone or something?"

"No. I'm standing there."

"Is anybody else with you or around you?"

"I don't know."

"Okay. What we're going to do is go to a significant time in this life of yours as this little boy. We'll go to a time when he is a little older. Find a meaningful time. I'll count to three and you'll be there and you will be able to describe it to me. One . . . two . . . three. Okay, what is happening?"

"There is nothing. It stops there. I think I die there. I don't . . . "

"You're a little boy in the pile again?"

"Yes. I think . . . I don't . . . "

"Okay . . . "

She began to get agitated. "I want to leave."

I saw no reason to proceed with this episode. "Go ahead and let the soul leave the body and travel up. I know it's confusing, but you'll be able to travel to the in-between state and when you get there, as you know, it will be peaceful. Go ahead now and travel there. Tell me when you get to the in-between state, the plane state."

She began to relax noticeably. "These women are here and they take me."

"Women are there?"

"Yes. There are two of them."

"In the in-between state?"

"Yes."

"Are you feeling better now?"

"Yes. It's so peaceful here."

"Good. Tell me about these women who are there. Are they your . . . " I had to stop myself from leading her. "Who are they?"

"They're showing me where to go so I won't be lost. I don't know if they are angels or guides or what. But they're gentle and they feel peaceful. They make me feel at peace . . . with everything."

"Okay. Just tell me what happens."

"They just seem to go into a corridor that's . . . it isn't the clouds. It's just . . . it's lit like sunshine. We seem to be going up like a spiral. I don't see a staircase, but just steps . . . and I sense there are other people there, but I don't see them. I'm not afraid."

"Tell me when you get to where you are going."

"It's just a big expanse. Just very serene."

"Okay. While we're in this tranquil place right now, in looking back . . . I know you were . . . you came from the body of a three-year-old boy. What lesson, if any, did that boy need to learn in his lifetime?"

"I don't know. It was like something was started and not finished. It was . . . there was . . . it was almost like being in the wrong place."

"Is any of that applicable to Carol in her present lifetime?"

"Well . . . she might be over her . . . burned out, not burned up. Over her head . . . too many responsibilities. I guess . . . I guess, lost in a sense. Maybe the burning . . . the burning of all the bodies . . . maybe that means something or its meaning is escaping me."

"What would that mean to Carol?"

"Not to get . . . not to throw herself on the pile."

"Okay . . . very good. Is there any, was there any particular purpose of this young boy's life?" She had seemed so sad throughout this life, I wasn't sure how she would answer.

"No," she answered quickly. "I think he was in the wrong life. He somehow slipped in . . . dropped in the wrong place."

"Could you tell me the young boy's name?"

"Deidre."

"What year was that? Approximately? What year or century did he come from?"

"Oh, I don't know. Long . . . I sense it was a long time ago . . . centuries ago. It was a desert. I don't think it was in the United States, but I couldn't see anything," she said almost apologetically. "It was just . . . "

"That's all right," I reassured her. "Any idea at all what land you think it might have been? Anything?"

"Maybe it *was* the West. I think there was a river some-where beyond the desert. But all I could see was the desert and the pile and the fire."

"Is there anything else you would like to relate to Carol or to anyone from the in-between state?"

"They said there is peace here."

I was pleased that she seemed so comfortable once again and felt that we could now proceed to return to her present lifetime. "What we are going to do now is to go back to the elevator to the body of Carol. I'm going to count to three and you will travel back to the elevator on the eighth floor. One . . . two . . . three. Let your soul travel back. Are you there in the elevator now?"

"Yes." She further relaxed noticeably.

"Push the button to go down to one . . . down there yet?"

She nodded.

"Now let's go into the garden . . . and again, let's rest in the garden . . . feeling very untroubled."

CAROL

Dr. Klein continued to bring me out of the hypnotic state. When I opened my eyes, I was silent for a moment. I had a thousand questions for him. What had happened when the telephone rang? I had felt confused . . . saw light . . . but it certainly validated Dr. Klein's claim that the subject always is in control and can hear extraneous sounds.

I felt as though I had seen more than I was able to report . . . the boy had dark straight hair and haunting dark brown eyes. There was something about the pile of bodies that I wanted to remember . . . but I didn't seem able to. There was more I wanted to acknowledge about the women in the in-between state, but the thoughts faded.

Although I was pleased that I was still able to go into the trance state after so long an absence, I felt a deep frustra-tion that there was more to tell if only I could remember it.

It bothered me greatly that I felt so strongly that Deidre had gotten into that life by mistake. What did that mean? Do we sometimes pop into a life by error? If so, do we die young and thus correct the mistake? Whose mistake is it? Is our soul overanxious to return or is there some cosmic confusion? I hoped Dr. Klein had time to answer all my questions. They were overwhelming.

DR. KLEIN

This regression and past-life experience was different from many others Carol had encountered. For one, the details and course of events were much more vague. There was a starkness permeating her words that matched that of the desert in which she found herself. The only prominent occurrence and focus was that of death itself.

The little boy Deidre was alone, lost, and thrown onto the pile. Interestingly, Carol at this time also felt somewhat alone and lost, trying to cope with and make sense of the tragic and untimely death of her best friend.

Sad times had befallen Carol regarding her friend's illness. Because of her background, she knew only too well and had known for months what the recurrence of this phase of the disease meant as far as a long-term prognosis. Juggling roles as interpreter between physicians and her friend, comforter, chauffeur, and sometimes cook, she was exhausting her own reserves, even as her friend's time on this earth was also running out.

Questions arose and Carol was questioning "the meaning of it all." Although becoming a believer in reincarnation, she still found it difficult to accept the loss of this loved one, especially after losing so many others in her life. As Deidre, the little boy in her past life died along with many on the pile, Carol knew that she, too, would soon have to face future deaths.

I believe the young boy's brief life and death occurred so

that she could more effectively and peacefully deal with those who had died in the past and who might die in the future. The soul will eventually enter a new body, a belief that is as hopeful as calming. As the guides—those familiar and comforting women—helped Carol to find peace in the in-between state, she could now find internal peace in this incarnation following the loss of her dear friend. In essence, she could separate herself from the pile and go on with life.

17

Return to a Life Once Visited

DR. KLEIN

We were now back on track. Although the issue of death was somewhat draining on Carol, she did feel relief and I could see that she was proceeding to work very well through her grief. Once again her energy was flowing.

Over the many months of working together, I had become very familiar with Carol's emotional peaks and valleys. I had seen her fatigued by illness and exhausted by other pressures, yet become impressed with her ability to "answer the bell" when challenged by work that stimulated her as she was with our project.

My own excitement with what had already transpired and with what still might occur was exhilarating. I looked forward to our next meeting, wondering what issues might be uncovered. However, much to my surprise, we proceeded to revisit a life that had presented itself during our initial work together over a year before.

Our proceedings had fallen into a particular pattern. Carol would arrive at my office and we'd spend forty-five minutes to an hour "warming up," just talking about current events, what was going on in her life, articles or books either of us had read, and so on. Then, I—she never initiated it—would suggest that we begin our work.

I'd fiddle with the cords to the tape recorder—partly because they seem to have the uncanny knack of rearranging themselves in knots from session to session and partly to give Carol a chance to sit down in the chair and to quiet herself. Something of a perfectionist, she was bothered by the thought that it "might not work."

But she was a good subject and, as almost always occurred, quickly slipped into a deep hypnotic state. Once she had entered through the door in the garden, I asked her to look down at her feet and to tell me what she saw.

"Shoes."

"What type of shoes?" I asked.

"I think they're boots," she answered immediately. "But it's hard to tell. It's dark."

"The clothes you have on. How would you describe them?"

She hesitated slightly. "Leather. Hunting-type clothes."

"Looking at your body and your face, are you a man or a woman?"

"A man," she said at once.

"About how old would you say you are?"

"I'm in my late twenties."

"Can you tell me your name at this point?"

"No," she said after a long pause. I knew it bothered her when she couldn't "see" a name, as she put it.

"Can you describe your surroundings to me?"

"It's a dark forest. The trees are close together and very tall." Now she spoke with no hesitation at all, reporting methodically and unemotionally what she was viewing.

"Just go ahead, walk a little, and tell me what's happening."

She gave a deep sigh. "I'm hunting. Small game."

"What are you hunting with?"

"Bow and arrow."

"Is this for sport? Or food?"

She answered spontaneously. "No, it's my job."

At this point, a car alarm from the parking lot below my office sounded. Carol jumped. "Just relax and remain where you are," I told her, hoping the alarm would cut off quickly. Fortunately, it did. "Go ahead," I said. "You were telling me about the game."

She hesitated. "I'm seeing lights ... I ... I've lost ... I can't see ... "

"Is it dark? What happened?"

"It's like a white light in my eye. I feel disconnected ... "

I realized immediately what had happened. Carol was slipping out of the hypnotic state. "It's okay. I'm going to help you," I said. "I'm going to count to three. Each number I count up, you will go deeper into trance, and when I reach three, you'll go to a very significant time in this man's life. You'll be able to get there. You'll be able to tell me what is happening ... " I counted slowly to give her more time to refocus. " ... One ... two ... three."

She had regained her concentration again. "I've come back to my house. There are soldiers around and they're lighting the thatched roof." Her voice became agitated as she spoke.

"They're lighting it?" I wasn't sure I had understood her correctly.

"They're lighting the thatched roof! They're setting it afire!" She sounded exasperated that I wasn't seeing the scene, too. It obviously was quite vivid to her.

"Tell me what happens."

"They're burning it down. And they're taking me away ... and they're taking my wife. They're taking us back. They say I've taken the game. I say it's not true."

It was déjà vu. She was reliving Arad's life. I have only experienced this a few times before during my patients' regressions. I tried to remain nonchalant, keeping my voice calm and shielding the excitement I felt. "Where are they taking you?"

"To a cellar and they separate us. I hear her screaming. They ask again what I've done with the game and I said I don't have ... I didn't take it. They take me into this room. There's a table with a stone above the table. They lash me down ... with my feet at one end and my arms at the other." Her voice filled with fear. "They're lowering the stone. They want me to confess."

"Go ahead. Tell me what's happening."

She began to gasp for breath. "They're lowering it. It's hard to breathe. And I told them it was ... I seem to ... " She was gasping now. I waited. Then she fell silent for at least ten seconds. Still I lingered. At last she spoke, so softly I had to strain to hear. "I look down. There's ... blood."

"Have you left your body? Have you died?"

"Yes."

"Travel to the in-between state," I told her. "Tell me when you get there."

"There's light ... warmth ... "

"Very good. Are any of the guides with you? There doesn't have to be."

"No," she answered. "I don't see anyone."

"What lessons did this man have to learn in his life?"

She spoke the words I had heard before. "Perhaps if he had spoken up sooner they might have just punished him and not killed him."

"How would this lesson be applicable in some way to Carol?"

"She's learning to speak up . . . to defend herself. To say the truth so she's not hurt."

"Is there another purpose or is this the only purpose of this man's life?"

"I think he wasn't loyal with his wife because he didn't speak up. The truth will protect those you love and not hurt them."

"Is there anything else you would like to relate from the in-between state? Any messages or anything that you would like to say to Carol or to myself or to anyone? Are any of the guides there now? They don't have to be."

"It's nothing to be frightened of. It's broad and roomy. It's not frightening."

Her respiration had begun to return to normal. "Okay," I said gently. "I'll let you now travel back . . . back through the door through space and into the garden. Are you back in the garden?" She nodded. "Good. Feeling very comfortable . . . very safe."

CAROL

I knew, even as I was speaking, that I was Arad, the hunter, once again. Although I had not reread or even glanced at any of my notes from last year's regressions, I nevertheless knew that the burning house was exactly as I had seen it before, as though I were watching reruns on the television screen. I also could feel the sting of the bowstring on my arm. The cellar of the castle where my wife and I were brought gave me the same cold and damp sensations I had previously experienced, and once again I felt the breath being squeezed out of me as the stone was lowered, crushing my chest.

I remember thinking, "Help me," as I was gasping and wondering why Dr. Klein hadn't taken me away from the experience. I had forgotten that I could have done the same thing myself.

DR. KLEIN

I found it most interesting that, after a year's passage of time, Carol went back to the life of Arad. Although not recalling specifics of her first regression to this lifetime, she readily spoke, almost identically and with similar emotion, about events that previously occurred. The question then is why did Carol choose to travel back to this particular period; what same issue was still unresolved?

Actually, my search didn't take too long as I was able to go back through my earlier notes. However, although clarity was provided and a reason obtained, I was also quite pleased with the regression itself. For it was my conviction that the close repetition of events could not, and would not, have occurred unless Carol actually had revisited this lifetime.

The revisit pointed out that Carol still needed to "speak up" and become increasingly more assertive. Recent family events created a need for her to step in, but doubts lingered for her as to what role she should assume. The question remained of how much or how little to involve herself.

Coincidence that she chose to reenter Arad's lifetime? I don't believe so. Now with this reinforcement, Carol could actively and appropriately intervene whenever needed.

18

KARMA FULFILLED

DR. KLEIN

*I*felt as though we were "on a roll." Our recent recess had in no way retarded our progress. We now were dealing successfully with two major concerns—assertiveness and coping with death. Carol's life was filled with a variety of activity and she now was capably putting everything in its proper place. Understanding of herself gave way to positive action; and this action, to resolution. Thus feeling confident with our gains, I saw her again the following week.

CAROL

I was enjoying our meetings again after so long a break.

Although I had worked on a few additional most interesting projects during our hiatus, I was fascinated by what I was discovering through these most recent regressions. It was as though I were both surgeon and subject, doing an emotional dissection. I felt most confident that Dr. Klein would allow me to "do no harm." It was with this upbeat attitude that I presented myself at his office to do yet another regression.

DR. KLEIN

The induction went smoothly and quickly this time. Although she was unable to see a door in the garden, she focused on an archway and felt comfortable stepping through it and into a past life. As before, I asked Carol to look down at her feet and to describe what she saw.

"Shoes . . . no, moccasins with hide laces that wrap around my legs."

"What type of clothes do you have on?"

"It's like a lambskin . . . long shirt . . . smock." She sighed.

"Are you a man or woman?"

"A boy."

"About how old are you?"

"About eight."

"Now look around you and describe what you see." I could see her eyes moving beneath her closed lids.

"I see hills, grass, a village off to the distance . . . "

"Is that where you live or . . . "

"Yes. I live there."

"Before we go to the village, though, tell me, what are you doing where you are right now? Are you playing or . . . what's happening?"

"I'm in charge of the sheep."

"I see. Are you taking care of the sheep for somebody?"

"My uncle."

"Do you enjoy your work as you're taking care of this?"

She cocked her head, considering her answer for a moment. "It's a good responsibility," she said at last. "It makes me feel proud."

"Very good. Now I'd like you to go to your home. Go back to the village where you're living. Can you find your home? I'm going to count to three and you'll be there. One . . . two . . . three. Can you describe your house to me? Your home?"

"It's made of stone . . . rocks, big boulders. There's one big room with a fireplace. There's a side room with . . . like a cloth that divides it. We eat in the big room. The children sleep there. It isn't totally closed. Part of it's open to the front. There's like . . . a skin flap that we drop down when the weather's bad. But usually it's up."

"Do you have parents or . . . who is in your family, your family members?"

"I live with my aunt and uncle and my grandmother. And I have cousins."

"What happened to your parents?"

"They were killed . . . they were drowned . . . I'm not sure how it happened."

"What land is this?"

"It's Greece," she said without hesitation.

"And the year?"

Her eyes fluttered as though she were trying to see something that would help her with the answer. Finally, she said, "I'm not sure of the year."

"That's okay," I reassured her. "What we're going to do . . . " Then I realized that I hadn't asked her name. "Oh, what do they call you?" She mumbled something. "I'm sorry. What's your name?" I repeated.

"I can't hear it," Carol answered.

"We'll find out your name another time. That's okay." It isn't unusual for subjects in regression to have difficulty recalling their name, or the date for that matter. I didn't want her inability to know her name to weaken her concentration. "What I'd like you to do now . . . when I count to three,

we're going to go to a very significant time in this lifetime of
yours. It could be either earlier than this original date or
later, but it will be a very important time. I'm going to count
to three and when I reach three, you'll be there. One ... two
... three. What's happening?"

"I'm in my late teens. I'm in a ... like a camp for young
men. We're training for warfare. It's my first time away from
home. I don't want the others to know I'm frightened."

"What's happening?"

"We're training ... fighting with sticks as though they are
spears. I'm afraid of being cut. There's an older man who's
instructing us. I trip and fall, and he makes fun of me and
the other boys laugh. I'm clumsy. I'm shy. I spend a lot of
time by myself. I'm embarrassed that I'm not as strong and
able as the other boys."

"What do they call you now? What is your name? What
do the other boys call you?"

"Dom."

"Dom?"

"Dom. Dominick, I guess, but they call me 'Dom.'"

"Okay, Dom. We're going to go to another time that's very
important in your life. When I count to three, you'll be there.
Another significant time in Dom's life. One ... two ... three."

There was a long pause. I didn't speak because it seemed
as though she was seeing something. I waited for her to report.

"I'm alone. I'm old. I have a lean-to on top of a hillside. I
think my wife has just died. I have no one. We have no children."

"You say 'just died.' Do you mean the last couple of days
or recently or just a couple of minutes ... "

"Recently. Couple of weeks, I guess."

"I see."

"And the villagers have all left. I just find myself very
alone."

"What did you do in your lifetime?"

"Well," he said somewhat defensively, "I fought in some battles." Then he admitted, "I wasn't a good soldier. Sometimes I hid. Then after that, I farmed, took care of sheep, married, but there wasn't good love there. I feel like I'm back where I started from."

"In what way?"

"I'm alone with the sheep."

"I see."

"I don't feel like I've progressed."

"Is there a city you're near? A port, maybe?"

"No, I'm still near that village."

"What's the name of the village?"

"Sprectka. Sprectka. It's near the Aegean."

I hoped we could pinpoint the location more specifically. "Is there another township or provinces near there?"

"No. I've never left."

"What about when you went to battle? Where did you go to for the fighting?"

"Neighboring villages along the sea."

"Were there any other townships that you recall?"

"Not that I can remember. I do remember wanting to go to sea after I left the fighting. But my uncle said there was work to do and I was needed. One of his sons was killed. He was much braver than I."

"Did he go to sea?"

"No, he died in the fighting."

"What were the armies called? Was there a name for the armies?"

"They weren't that organized."

"What was that?"

"We weren't that organized."

"Oh, I see. Who was in charge of the armies?"

"I can't think of his name. He was a big man with a beard."

"All right. What I'd like to do now is to take you to the time just before your death, a time you'll be able to tell me about. About five minutes or so before. And then we'll proceed to the death so that the soul can leave the body and go to the in-between state. I'm going to count to three. One . . . two . . . three. Can you tell me what's happening?"

"I've fallen . . . fallen on the path. I tripped over a rock or something. I think I've broken a bone. I'm old. My bones are fragile. I can't . . . I crawl for help, but there's no one there. I try to drag myself down the path, but I don't think I can make it."

"Okay. Let the body die. Allow the soul to leave the body and travel to the in-between state. Just tell me when you get there."

" . . . All right."

"In looking back at Dom's life, what lesson did he need to learn?"

"To act . . . to stand up for himself. To have dreams and not let others decide his life. It was a wasted life."

"So he didn't have any dreams?"

"His only dream was that he wanted to go to sea, but he didn't pursue it. He didn't push. He was very passive," she said disgustedly.

"How would that be applicable to Carol?"

"I think she's had to make things happen in her life. Not to just wait until . . . to have dreams and even though others didn't share them, to have them, believe in them, and make them happen."

"Was there a particular purpose to Dom's life?"

"Well . . . he really didn't put meaning for anyone. Not his wife, not his relatives, not even the other men he fought with. He was just there . . . taking up space."

"Is there any message from this in-between state that you want to have for Carol or anyone?"

"Only that you can't move forward without putting one foot in front of the other." She chuckled. "Every time he tried, he fell . . . but you have to have a goal and even if you don't reach it, you've had it. Sometimes the excitement is in the chase."

"Are there any of the guides with you at this time?"

"Yes."

"Do they want to say anything?"

"No, they're ... carrying me ... surrounding me. They tell me that you must push and to reach out."

"Was there anybody in Dom's life who is in Carol's life? Who travels with her?"

"No, I really don't see any of the faces clearly enough to know."

"Okay. Very good. What we're going to do now is to return back to the garden through the arch. Let your soul travel back ... coming back to the garden through the arch you entered before. Back to the body of Carol. Are you there now?"

"Yes."

"Just rest comfortably ... "

CAROL

I roused from the trance state feeling ... "cheated" is the best word, I think. I don't understand why I felt such loathing—and not pity—for Dom. But I do know that I did not like him. Not only was he passive, but he was disloyal. He admitted that he often had hidden in battle. He entered into a loveless marriage, didn't pursue his dream of going to sea, and even *he* didn't think much of his life.

Later, I looked up Greece in the *World Book Encyclopedia*. I discovered that in ancient Greece, boys as young as seven were sent to military camps to be trained for battle. Perhaps that was where young Dom learned to fight.

Dr. Klein reminded me that Dom was not me, that he was a past life, and that I obviously had "improved" on some of Dom's failings. Unfortunately, I had scheduled another appointment too tightly and had to leave his office before we could talk out my feelings and feel some closure, as we usually had done.

DR. KLEIN

Not since Hans was Carol so upset with one of her previous lives. Suffice to say that during the regression and immediately afterward, the common denominator was disgust.

Carol in this lifetime loathed what Dom was all about: not because of his lack of physical strength, but that he remained passive and let others make decisions for him. With surprising (and seldom seen) anger Carol continued to lament the fact that she lived such a life.

Finally, after much venting, she calmed down and began to converse. Actually, I tried to convey to her that she had learned Dom's lessons well and that her karma was being fulfilled. She dreams and is a dreamer; she has visions. Whereas Dominick fell and couldn't move forward, Carol loves the excitement of the chase and is willing to try; she will make things happen.

However, I soon realized that I wasn't getting through. Although she was listening, Carol's mind was elsewhere. Anger and disgust concerning Dominick remained. Another day would have to come before Carol could or would hear me. And, as we left my office, walking down the hall, she continued to fume and mumble about the wastefulness of Dominick's life—not seeing anything but her own anger.

19

A Lost Love

CAROL

*B*oth of us had been extremely preoccupied with work which precluded our getting together to discuss what I called "my wasted life." I understood it centered around a recurring issue for me: lack of assertiveness. The day I returned to Dr. Klein's office, I said, "I can't wait for my next life to see if I finally settled the assertiveness issue in this one." I was partly joking and partly serious.

As expected, Dr. Klein put the ball in my court, asking, "Well, what do you think?"

Obviously, I had done some thinking about it because I felt as though I knew the answer. "I think I have resolved it," I said. "I've finally learned how to speak out without being aggressive, how to make my thoughts and needs known." I laughed. "So I guess I don't have to hurry on to the next life to find out."

Because we both were somewhat pressed for time, we had little small talk, but quickly settled in for the search for another past life. Although I was totally familiar with the induction, I still seemed to need the ritual to help me focus my concentration so that I could go into the alpha state.

But to my extreme frustration, extraneous sounds kept interfering. Once again I heard the garbage truck's warning horn outside from the parking lot below. How many times a week did they get their garbage picked up? I thought angrily. A door closed; there was the sound of running water. I don't know if Dr. Klein was aware of it, but I couldn't seem to empty my mind or direct my attention. I squirmed in the chair, trying to get more comfortable. Then, unexpectedly, my eyelids drooped. I felt myself feeling lighter . . . a floating sensation . . . and Dr. Klein's low calm voice counting backward.

DR. KLEIN

I didn't realize that Carol was somehow distracted. I was caught up in something else that I could not—and still cannot—explain. As was my usual practice, I turned on the tape recorder as soon as I began the induction. But this time, for some reason, I reached into my drawer and pulled out a hand-held recorder. Quickly, I inserted the miniature tape and clicked it on. Now we were recording the session on two separate tape recorders.

Once again, Carol seemed lost in the garden and was unable to see any doors. She complained about "too much light" blinding her. This meant to me that she felt a reluctance to leave the garden, which she had come to know as a safe place. Once again, to overcome her resistance, I switched to the elevator induction. She calmly entered the elevator, then murmured something about "too many buttons."

"Just choose one," I told her. "Push whichever button you want."

She shrugged slightly and said. "Eight. I pushed the eighth button."

When she told me she had arrived on the eighth floor, I asked her to step out of the elevator and look down at her feet. She reported seeing black shoes. "And what kind of clothes do you have on?"

"It's a black dress with long sleeves," she said in a quiet voice. "It's buttoned up to the neck."

"Look at your body. Tell me about your face and hair. What type of hair do you have?"

"It's coal black. It's piled up on the back of my head."

"What is your name?"

"Elizabeth."

"Elizabeth, where are you? What town or city or country are you in?"

Her eyes fluttered. "There's water . . . a coast, big rocks . . . They're black."

"What country is that?"

"America."

"In what state?"

"It's New England."

"By the way, can you tell me the year or what century this is?"

"I'm not sure."

"That's okay. It's all right. Elizabeth, I'd like you to look around you and tell me what you see." She didn't begin speaking, so I added, "Go for a walk and describe what is happening."

"There's wild flowers. I'm walking out to the point. Here there's water as far as I can see."

"About how old are you now, Elizabeth?"

"Late thirties . . . "

"What we're going to do now, Elizabeth, is we're going to

go to a very significant time in your life. It could be before or after your thirties. I'm going to count to three and when I reach three, you will be there—and you can tell me what's occurring at that time. It will be a very important and significant time in your life. One . . . two . . . three. What's happening?"

She frowned slightly. "I'm in . . . a large room. It used to be the living room of a large house. Now it's filled with beds. There's dying all around me. I'm helping to care for the young men. But I really don't know what I'm supposed to be doing."

"Are you like a nurse? Or a . . . some other type of helper?"

"I'm not a nurse, but I'm administering to their needs. There are doctors here who tell me what I'm supposed to do."

"I see. About how old are you now?"

"Seventeen."

"What's happening? Go ahead and describe it to me."

Her eyes looked around under closed lids. "There's moaning . . . moaning all around. They've turned this house into a care station. Some of the men are so young. My age."

"Why are they there? What's happened? What's been going on?"

She looked sad. "They've been in battle. They've been injured."

"What war is this?" She hesitated. "What do they call it?" I asked.

"The war for independence."

"Is there anything else happening at this time?"

"I sit and read to some of them, bring them water, help feed them, change their dressings. They have grievous wounds." There was a long pause. "I don't know why I have such an overwhelming urge to help and protect them."

"I understand." She seemed to disconnect with that aspect of her life, so I decided it was time to move on. "Elizabeth, what I'd like to do now is to go to another important time in your life. I'm going to again count to three and when I reach three, you'll be there and begin to tell me what happens." I counted and waited without prompting.

At last she began to speak. "I'm sitting in my room, writing. I'm writing a poem . . . it's about love," she added shyly.

That surprised me. "It's about love? How old are you . . . or about how old are you? Do you know?"

"My mid-twenties."

"Are you in love with somebody or is this just about love in general?"

"No, I do love somebody . . . but he's gone away." Her voice trembled with emotion.

"Who was he?"

"He's a merchant on a ship. He said . . . he promised that he'd return. But he hasn't. He said we'd be together again. But it's been two years. I've waited for his return."

"Okay. Elizabeth, there's been two periods of time that you've told me about. Let's go to a third. A very important time in your life." Once again, I counted to three to give her time to move on to another significant period in her life. "What's happening?" I asked as she remained silent.

"I'm waiting. Waiting for the ship to return."

"Has it returned?"

"He had come back once. And then he left. Afterward, I learned that I was carrying his child. He must come back," she said with panic in her voice. "I can't face the others."

"Does he come back?"

She hesitated. "No," she said softly.

"What do you do?"

"I live with my brother. I can't tell him. I can't tell him what's happened. I'm frightened. I walk up to the point. The water is crashing against the rocks below. My poems are in the box at home. They'll find them and they'll know what happened. But it won't matter any more. I walk back to the path, trying to choose. I sit down on a rock and begin to unlace my boots." She laughed gently. "I don't know why I don't want to get them wet. I let my hair down. The wind's in my face. And I run. It's like I'm flying. I just run. I seem to float as I go off the cliff . . . "

"What happens?"

"I can smell the salt air as I fall. Then I must hit my head. I see myself fallen, my form and crumpled dress beating against the rocks by the sea."

"Allow your spirit to leave your body." Then I reconsidered my statement. "It sounds as though it already has. So let your soul travel to the in-between state. Let me know when you get there." She murmured that she had. "Do you have any reflections? What lessons did Elizabeth need to learn from this life?"

"She kept her thoughts on paper. She didn't speak her mind. She let others live her life, let the man she loved slip through her fingers. He went out to sea. When he came back, she let him slip through again."

"What should she have learned from that?"

"She should have told him what he meant to her. She kept her life so within. You need to reach out with energy and the positive . . . has to reach out. It's like what you call a fire brigade passing a bucket from hand to hand. The positive energies are passed along from one to another. If the chain is broken, it delays the outcome. We must reach out to connect."

"How would this be applicable to Carol?"

"She's opening; she's reaching out, connecting. Passing along the positive energy. It multiplies. It's not one and one, then two, then three. Rather it's one, then two, then four, eight, sixteen . . . "

"While you're in the in-between state," I said, "how is the soul of Elizabeth now after the suicide? What's going to happen to your soul now?"

"She killed both herself and her unborn child. Those two souls are interconnected. They travel together to make their peace."

"When will she go back into another body . . . I shouldn't say 'she.' When will the soul go back into another body?"

"After it has learned more, it will go back."

"If there is what?" She was speaking so softly, it was difficult to hear.

"There are lessons to be learned before going back. But it will. Many times, as it has done before . . . until all the connections are made."

She sounded as though she were speaking someone else's thoughts here. The guides, perhaps? "Okay," I said, making notes. "Very good. Are the guides there? Do they want to tell you anything?"

"I've been told to share the energy. It flows from within and exudes out. It is expressed in different ways, in different lifetimes. The body's the receptor, the conductor, the means of expressing energy in life . . . " Her voice faded off. She seemed very tired.

"Let the soul travel back, back to the body of Carol. Back to the elevator on the eighth floor . . . " Slowly, gently, I began to help her find her way back. " . . . back to the garden, back to your safety . . . comfort . . . "

CAROL

This regression seemed strange in many ways. I felt disconnected somehow. The scene in the living room where I helped to nurse the soldiers seemed out of focus, as though I were viewing it through a scrim, a gauze-like curtain. I watched Elizabeth as a young girl helping to care for the young soldiers, but unlike other regressions where I could report to Dr. Klein what I was *doing,* in this scene I was reporting what I saw Elizabeth doing. The vagueness of it all was disturbing.

The reality, for me, was on the cliff at what Elizabeth called "the point." I knew without any doubt that I had once sat there, perhaps for hours, perched on one of the massive boulders that lined the path, just staring out to sea. I have visualized that scene many times in this life and only realize, as I write these words, that it is so. Just as I felt myself squinting to keep out the sun, I knew the sensation of the wind from the sea blowing through my hair when I let it down, making it dance around my head. My cheeks burned from the ever-present sea breeze. My lungs filled hungrily with the salt air.

Although Elizabeth was eventually to die at that locale, I found that site to be one of calm, peace, and security. I think Elizabeth wandered there often, waiting for her merchant seaman to return. That he did return once must have given her great joy—and perhaps is why she allowed herself to be wooed and left pregnant by him.

As Elizabeth, I felt not despair, but rather an overwhelming sadness with my two unpleasant choices—to have my lover's baby out of wedlock and suffer humiliation and possible rejection from friends and family or to give up and jump to my death. The latter seemed easier. Elizabeth was unable to share her thoughts or problems with others. That was why the strongbox of which she spoke was filled with poems—all unpublished. She was able to unburden herself only by putting pen to paper. Her only confidant was her stationery, a trait I shared for many years in this life.

DR. KLEIN

Fascinating! Once again the unexplained reared up, catching me by surprise. For, as I mentioned earlier, without any particular reason, I reached for a second tape recorder at the beginning of the regression—something I had never done previously with anyone. Then afterward, with wonderment and awe, I sat startled as I tried to play back the tape from my primary recorder. What I heard was silence, interspersed with bits of phrases and high-pitched sounds. Fortunately, our session had been safely preserved on the auxiliary tape. Why did I turn on a backup recorder for this session? I don't know—but I'm glad I did.

As a result of this regression, Carol once again received reinforcement for becoming and remaining more assertive. She is now solidified in the knowledge that she needs to speak up and reach out in order to achieve her desires. With a degree of sadness, she saw how Elizabeth, by remaining silent and passive, suffered the loss of her lover.

Elizabeth, unfortunately, chose to kill herself. Not only did she die, but her unborn child died with her. I believe that the paths of these two souls then became intertwined, and they will have to travel together through time until they make their peace.

Carol recognized her boyfriend, the seafaring merchant during the life of Elizabeth, as being her husband in this incarnation. Soul mates, they have been trying to resolve their relationship through the ages. Having been abandoned by the merchant while pregnant in her previous life, she has now been happily married for many years. Interestingly, as one might expect, they have decided to enjoy a large family. It appears that this time around resolution has occurred.

20

THE HEALER

DR. KLEIN

*A*s I sat and allowed my mind to wander, reflecting on Carol's many lives, a restful contented feeling floated through me. Not only did I feel elated about what we had accomplished, but I was anxiously awaiting the opportunity to share all that we had done and learned with others.

In part, I felt some sadness that we wouldn't continue on, but I knew the time had come to concentrate on finishing with the regressions so that we could focus our efforts on completing the manuscript. Still though, I was glad to see that Carol had scheduled for later in the week.

CAROL

As Dr. Klein readied the tape recorder, I had my usual fear that I wouldn't be able to go into the hypnotic state. I guess I considered that possibility to be some type of failure. I know that I often procrastinated, avoiding taking my seat by asking him questions he would feel obligated to answer. I voiced my concern, and he assured me that it wasn't an uncommon one.

He dimmed the lights and I leaned back in the chair, my feet comfortably propped up on the footstool. As he began speaking, I was very conscious again of the beeping warning horn of a garbage truck as it backed up somewhere outside. I can't focus, I thought to myself. It's not going to work. But I must have been concentrating so intently on the sound of Dr. Klein's voice that almost immediately I felt the familiar lightness flow over me like warm sea water. Then, he was asking me to look for the door in the garden. There was only one this time, a massive wooden one turned black with age.

DR. KLEIN

I asked Carol to step through the wooden door and, once on the other side, to look down at her feet and tell me what she saw.

"I'm barefoot," she exclaimed.

"What are you wearing?"

She hesitated, then answered, "Fur."

"What does it cover?"

Again, she hesitated. "It goes over one shoulder. It comes down to the calves of my legs."

"Look around at your surroundings," I requested. "Could you describe them to me?"

"It's very rocky. Sharp, sharp rocks. Mountainous. Some green, but the rocks are very sharp."

"Go to the place that you live . . . Are you there?"

"Yes," she answered.

"Can you describe it to me, please?"

She spoke without any hesitation, reporting what she was seeing unemotionally and fluently. "It's a cave within the rocks. It stretches back and divides into different chambers. The ground is dark. There are animal skins in some of the areas used for sleeping. The roof is low. The ground is hard . . . as you go farther back, it's harder to stand up."

"I see. About how old are you now?"

She paused, as though to consider. "Year wise young, but I . . . I feel old."

"Why is that?"

"I'm not sure."

"What is your name? What do they call you?"

"I'm not sure about that either," she said, frowning slightly.

"Where are you? What land is this?"

"I think it's . . . I think it's what we call Asia. It's . . . I don't recognize the name."

"Okay. Are you a boy or girl? Man or woman?"

"I'm a man."

"Young man? Old man?"

Again, she wrestled with my question. "I think I'm middle age for my time."

I wasn't sure I understood what she was saying, so I asked her to repeat what she had said.

"I'm in my middle years . . . "

" . . . for your time," I added.

"For my time," she agreed.

"Do you have a family?"

"No. I don't have a family. I belong to the tribe. I'm deformed. There's a . . . I see a thick, deformed foot. My back is burrowed."

I made note of her odd choice of the word "burrowed," but as she seemed fluent in her descriptions, I didn't want to interrupt her flow of words by asking what it meant. "Do you have any friends?"

"I sense that I'm liked. I'm The Healer," she said simply. "I belong to the tribe."

"You belong to the tribe?"

"Yes," she said.

"What is the name of the tribe?"

There was a long pause as she struggled to pronounce the name. "Oo Long," she answered at last. "Oo Long. I take care of them when they hurt, when they're injured."

"What happened to you that you have the deformities as you noted? Were you born that way?"

She responded without pause. "Yes, I was born that way. And they say that my mother died giving birth and my difference made me their healer. They don't shun me," she hastened to add.

"We're going to go now to a very important time in your life. It may be before the age you are now or later, but it will be very significant for you. When I count to three, you'll be there and you'll be able to describe to me what is occurring and be able to tell me readily what is going on. One . . . two . . . three. What's happening?"

Once again, she spoke quickly and spontaneously as though trying to keep up with the scene unfolding before her eyes. "We're in a clearing and one of the chief's wives is about to give birth, but the baby's stuck and the women come and ask my help. Men do not look upon giving birth," she said with disdain, "but the chief implores me and so I go. She is very young and is frightened. I know that I must deliver a healthy baby for her. But this is woman's work and I ask to be shown . . . I ask the gods to show me how, and they whisper in my ear and tell me what to do.

"I put my hands into a bowl of animal fat so that my hands are slippery and I chant to relax her. And with the women looking on, I carefully put my hands on the sides and slip them inside to feel the baby. The head is to the side and the cord is wrapped around the baby's head. I push each hand on each side of the womb to make it bigger and with my fingers work the cord around the baby's head. I push and try to turn the baby so that the head is unlodged and can fall in place." I could see Carol's fingers moving as she described what she, as The Healer, was doing.

"The girl is in great pain," she continued. "I chant and the women chant. I turn the baby and pull and, at last, the head comes through and slips . . . the body slips into my hands. I hand the baby to one of the women and back away."

"Very good," I praise. Then, "What happens next?"

"The chief is very pleased. He gives me the choice kill and honors me. All revere me as 'The Man Who Delivered the Baby.' "

"What do they call you?"

"Healer."

"Do you have a name besides that?"

She paused for the first time in many minutes, cocked her head as if to listen, and said, "I don't hear anything . . . "

"Healer, what year is this?"

"I have no judge of that."

"Do they call it . . . in your tribe, how do they designate time?"

"It's called the Fourth Summer, but . . . there are segments. They're not years, it's like segments. The Fourth Summer of . . . twelve segments."

"We want to go, Healer, to one other time that is very important for you. When I count to three, we'll be at another significant time in your life and you'll be able to describe it to me just as you did this one. One, two, three. What's happening?"

"My chief is lying on a bed of furs and he's dying. I am saddened that I can't help him. He is bleeding and the life pours out of him. I don't know how to stop the flow. I press on his groin with my knee and the flow stops somewhat. But he's weakened and the soups I make, the broth I bring . . . he weakens and soon dies."

"What happens to you? What do you do next?"

"I feel disgraced that I couldn't save him."

"What do you do?" I asked.

"I leave. I walk, follow the path until it ends. And still I keep walking. I sleep unprotected, and I don't search for food. I pass by waterfalls, but do not drink. I should have prayed for more knowledge and the gods would have answered, but I thought myself too wise."

"We're going to go now to the time of your death, when The Healer dies. You'll be able to describe to me what happens just before your physical body perishes. Then, when the actual death occurs, the soul can be released to go into the in-between state." I counted to three, then asked, "What's happening?"

"It's the end of the walk. I myself am too weakened and have no strength to go on, even if I cared to, which I don't. I'm ready to join my chief."

"Okay, let the body die and the soul be released. Allow the soul to travel to the in-between state. When you get there, let me know." There was a long pause. "Are you there now?"

"Yes," she answered.

I waited for that familiar look of peacefulness to come over her face before proceeding. Then I asked, "In looking back at the life of The Healer, what lesson did he need to learn?"

"Humility. That there's always more to learn. You need only to ask."

I began writing notes as my thoughts flowed rapidly, one after another. Yet, as I did not want her to lose focus, I asked quickly, "How would that be applicable to Carol in her life?"

"She will . . . will ask many on how to heal and will have . . . will learn humility."

"Is there anything else? Any messages for Carol or anyone? How might this be applicable?" I was eager to hear the answer.

"To interview new areas. You can't know your boundaries

if you don't try to reach. Just as The Healer turned the baby, you can turn other things around and make them work out. You have to heal The Healer."

"Is there any particular purpose of The Healer's life?" I asked. "I know you've mentioned several that sound like it, but is there any other purpose you might think of?"

"I think he was part of the plan to help people be born when they're to be born and to die when they're to die. He was an intermediary, trained by the gods, taught by the gods. And he returned to the gods."

"He was taught by the gods?" I repeated, to make certain I had heard correctly.

"Yes, they told him what to do."

"Very good. Are there any, where you are, in your space now, are there any of your guides or masters? . . . "

"Yes . . . "

"There are? Could you tell me . . . "

"Two, on either side," she answered.

"What's that?"

"There's one on either side. There's two of them."

"Do you want to talk to them? Do they want to talk to you? Ask them anything . . . ?"

"They say I'll return many times to heal. I've seen them before," she added matter-of-factly.

"Is there anything else you wish to tell me? Or they wish to tell?"

"No, they're just very . . . not protective . . . very soothing with me. I feel as though they're training me for something."

"Excellent. Is there anything else? If not, we can return to the garden." I paused to see if more was to be added. When she remained silent, I said, "Okay . . . let your soul travel back in space and time, back to the garden, back through the dark wooden door and into the garden. Are you back there now?"

"Yes."

"Again, the bright light of safety, the bright light there encompasses you, makes you feel very safe. Just enjoy the feeling . . . "

CAROL

As always, I'm shaken by the most vivid impression that I'm reporting a movie or taking part in an interactive one. The feeling that The Healer was part of an Oriental people somewhere in Asia engulfed me. After some research, I discovered that in the Philippines there was a place called "Olongapo." Perhaps this was where The Healer's Oo Long tribe resided. My further investigation revealed this area to indeed be not only mountainous—as I had reported from within the hypnotic state—but also to be filled with "sharp, dark, volcanic rock," almost the very same words I had used to describe it. Was this The Healer's homeland?

More important, I felt a strong kinship with The Healer, as though I were "inside" his skin. I knew his deformity; was that possibly from what I've experienced in this life because of various illnesses? Are his clubbed foot and bent back symbols of something I should understand, the meaning of which still escapes me?

His healing powers seemed so natural and expected, as well as his being completely accepted by his tribe. I fully identify with his pain at being unable to cure his chief as I, too, have lost some of those I loved and respected. Like him, I, too, have accepted blame though no one was accusing.

Often in this life others have said, "You make me feel so much better just by the way you listen," or "People seem drawn to you," and then jokingly add, "You must have healing powers." Is this an echo from my past?

As a young woman, I wanted to be a physician but was discouraged by my (male) internist. Was it only a coincidence, then, that my writing subjects over the years have gradually turned to those of a health care nature? Have I in some way been preparing for this career over the centuries?

Have I learned specific lessons enabling me to serve in this life as a medical liaison between physicians and their patients, a communicator? Lastly, have I learned The Healer's lesson, that of humility?

These questions and many more flood my mind—questions without answers. I wish I could go back and find The Healer once again. Although he is with me from my past, I feel a longing to learn more.

DR. KLEIN

At last—it happened. A past life I felt, no, that I *knew* had to have occurred finally surfaced. Never did I discuss this with Carol as I didn't want to influence her in any way. However, I was convinced that, somewhere in one of her previous lives, she had been faced with the challenge of helping people. When successfully achieved, karma would be fulfilled. Now we saw it: "The Healer" was the source.

Although I expected such a lifetime existed, it was thrilling to see and hear the actual occurrence. With great satisfaction and joy I listened intently as portions of The Healer's life unfolded.

While not a physical hands-on healer in this lifetime, Carol has been blessed with a talent that helps to heal in another manner. She creates, she writes, and not at all surprisingly she has chosen the medical field as her area of specialization.

Carol has learned well the lessons of The Healer: That there is always more to learn; you need only to ask. She does ask, she does learn, and then imparts her knowledge through the books she writes, helping to heal in this manner. Interestingly, as The Healer was told: "To interview new areas. You can't know your boundaries if you don't try to reach." Carol has tried so-called unchartered waters. She has been willing to reach out, explore, and search. Her boundaries have now been expanded and seem limitless.

EPILOGUE

CAROL

*I*t is now the fall of 1994. It's been more than a year thus far—eighteen months, to be exact—since I began the past-life regression project with Dr. Klein. What I expected to be no more than just another writing assignment—albeit an interesting one—has changed my life in so many ways that I could not list them all.

I've learned the answers to flashes of memories that have haunted me since early childhood, that precious period before we cross the river of forgetfulness which erases all recollections of previous lives. Even as a very small child, I had a recurring dream in which I lay in an iron bed, one of many in a long hall-like room. A giant hand reached down through the ceiling to pluck me up out of the bed. Surprisingly, I remember that this dream was not a frightening one, but rather one that comforted me. I dreamed it often until I reached my teen years. Then it was no more.

Not until I relived my life in Victorian England did I finally understand that my childhood dream was, indeed, a whisper from the past, a forgotten memory of the housemaid, Anna May, who died of consumption in one of the many iron beds that lined the women's ward of a temporary hospital in Birmingham.

An obvious transformation in my life has been the loss of a former fear of heights. I now find myself scampering up scaffolding and ceiling-hugging walkways in auditoriums, and flying in airplanes in total relaxation and comfort. Remembering—through my first regression—the experience of falling to my death in a past life has seemingly erased any anxiety I previously experienced in this one.

In retrospect, mulling over the many lives I have recalled, I am struck by several specific revelations. Although I consider myself to be a "cave dweller," content to live indoors and, for the most part, enclosed in small spaces, the majority of my past lives seem to have been lived in the vast out-of-doors. I was a hunter, a fisherman, a cowboy, and a healer who literally operated in the open.

Not only did I seem to have an affinity for the wide, open spaces, but in the majority of my past lives I was male. It seems to me, however, that the lives in which I was a woman tended to be happier and more fulfilling lives. I'll have to run that theory by Dr. Klein.

I'm honest enough (and vain enough, too) to admit that I had secretly hoped that I might find myself to be someone—not famous, necessarily, but at least well known. I think most of us would like to feel that there could have been a Michelangelo, Queen Victoria, or Lewis Carroll in our past. Alas, my only major successes seemed to have been as a first-class chambermaid and a holistic medicine man.

Reviewing my reading, I have learned that we travel with many of the same people throughout our lives. I think that this particular concept explains how we are immediately drawn to a stranger from "across a crowded room." It also would account for the feeling we get of being turned off by someone we have only met. Why would we reject a person at first sight unless he or she had been an antagonist in a former life?

I personally have found soul mates in past lives whom I know were or are with me now in this present life. I have traveled throughout the centuries with my brother, sister, sons, daughters, and husband and have been able to recognize them all during different regressions. I'll confess that my expectations were that I would have identified Dr. Klein as a teacher or mentor somewhere in one of the many past lives I experienced. I didn't or perhaps just didn't recognize him if he did appear in a particular lifetime.

Although there are other specific examples of changes that have taken place as a direct result of my past-life regressions, I think there is a far more complex, global, and overwhelming response.

As I reported just nine months into this project, my general attitude is different. I find myself more accepting—both of people and events—understanding that there are lessons to be learned from all experiences. I feel myself wrapped in the robe of peace, glowing from an inner light. I sense a purpose—my soul's purpose—and am content to let it be revealed to me at the proper time. I agree with Edgar Cayce who said that all human beings have much greater powers than they are ever aware of. I sense these powers growing as individuals seek me out to describe their own unusual personal experiences that they don't as yet comprehend.

When I was ten, I recall telling an adult friend of the family that "I have read a prayer that will guide my life." She smiled slightly, as adults often do when trying to react properly to the seriousness of a child, yet answered gravely, "You are lucky to have found your guide so young in life."

The prayer read as follows:

"Teach me, O Lord, to obey Thy will. To be content with that which Thou in Thy wisdom hast allotted to me, and to share my gifts with those who need my help."

I didn't know then why I memorized any prayer or why it was that particular one out of so many others. I didn't know what possessed me to declare so openly that it was to be such an important prayer to me. But it did direct the conduct of both my teen and adult years. I now know that those words were selected for me by my guides, the two tall women who have been with me throughout my lives. My work today is really no different than it was centuries ago for me when I was known as "The Healer" and lived in the mountains of the Philippines, administering to those who needed help.

There is great truth in the words of Joseph Conrad who said that the mind of a human being is capable of anything because everything is in it. We need only to focus on what we have learned from our past and to build on it, so that learning flows into knowledge, knowledge into learning, woven together by time so that soon no seam is revealed.

Just as Edgar Cayce made no more differentiation between the dead and the living than between the caterpillar, the cocoon, and the butterfly, past-life regression has taught me that life is like dawn and dusk, and that it often depends upon where you stand to know just when one entity is gone and another appears. While in some ways I am anxious to turn my attention to the beginnings of exciting new writing assignments, I find myself lingering with this one, basking in its warmth and feeling great reluctance to say "goodbye" to it. I sense that, unlike other creative ventures in which I could totally immerse myself in a particular topic during the research, writing, and promotional period, and then move on like a fickle lover to the next commitment, the *Soul Search* project is different. I am Pygmalion who has become enchanted with the sculpture. It has become an inherent part of me, who I am now, and what I am yet to become. I cannot escape what I have learned, nor do I have any desire to do so. What I have uncovered through this unlikely odyssey that began by seeming chance is the discovery of the continuation of the soul and the certainty that it will live on long after my physical body is no more.

If, knowing then what I know now, would I still agree to take part in the experiment? Would I willingly undergo past-life regressions to see where I have been in order to understand where I now am headed? Even if I realized how much I would be changed? My answer must be an overwhelming yes. My search is more directed, less fearful, and I am comforted by the knowledge that I am not alone.

Yet, most strangely, I feel no need to seek out converts to my truth. It is enough that I believe. Through my thoughts, words, and actions, the energies created by this belief reach out to others in a way that once seemed almost mystic, but now seems so natural to me. I know that others have been touched; our souls connect.

As Hillel said over two thousand years ago: "If I am not for myself, who will be for me? If I am only for myself alone, what am I? If not now, when?"

The answer, of course, is *now.*

DR. KLEIN

In the spring of 1992, when Carol and I first began to work together, I wasn't quite sure what would unfold. Quite aware of the power and efficacy of past-life therapy, I knew the potential that existed. However, once it was begun, I wondered whether Carol, who on the surface wanted to further learn and explore, would really desire to reveal some of her innermost thoughts in anything as public as a book.

Happily, as we proceeded, I was quite pleased with our progress and enjoyed observing Carol's continued growth.

She, as I've noted throughout, changed—not for change's sake, nor just to say that she'd changed—but that she genuinely became a woman with improved understandings and behaviors. Ironically, however, this newly acquired knowledge brought about its own difficult decision.

Because of both our jointly agreed use of the tape recorder for our sessions and Carol's high journalistic standards, a complete and accurate portrayal of her discoveries was honestly recorded. But, as has been seen within these pages, not all that was revealed was pleasant for Carol to learn and acknowledge, nor, more important, was it always solely about her. Hence, what to do?

Carol was torn. Should she publicly make herself known so that others could identify with her and share personally with her beliefs, or should she remain anonymous so as not to cause possible pain and embarrassment for those close to her by acknowledging personal problems?

For many days and weeks, Carol wrestled with this dilemma. She sought not only my advice, but also that of friends and family members with whom she felt she could confide. Finally, after agonizing over her decision, she determined that, at least for the present, she would remain anonymous and her name would not be listed on the book we had jointly written. However, we agreed to leave open the option for her to change her mind in the future.

Once this conflict was resolved, Carol was able to revel in the success of our completed work. Reflecting on her fourteen past lives, she noted that six were of women and eight were of men. The two remaining experiences included the one in which she had gone directly into the pre-birth state of her present life and the "re-visit."

The periods of time in which she lived ranged from 450 B.C., 65 B.C., 520 A.D., 1116, the 1500s, the 1600s, the late 1700s, the 1800s, and early 1900s to her birth in this life. The countries lived in included Africa, ancient Greece, Egypt, Holland, England, the former Soviet Union near the Ural

Mountains, the Philippines, Italy, and the United States. She had guides—usually women—who lovingly stayed with her in the "in-between state" and who supported, comforted, and advised her, although they did not appear in every past-life experience.

Carol, through it all, developed and became a woman much more satisfied with herself. She truly feels different—in the most positive sense—as she has revealed throughout this book. And still she marvels at the relative brevity of our work together. At times she admits that she is amazed, but very content, with that which has transpired.

Past-life therapy, although "around" for years, is still looked upon with awe and questions, even now during this last decade of the twentieth century. In my work with Carol and numerous others, I have known both the success and the joy it can bring.

I hope that many will hear the message this book offers, causing additional qualified therapists to begin utilizing this method to help those in need. There yet is much that needs to be learned, but with increasing numbers experiencing past lives, more will be learned. The prevailing rigidity of thought will soften. The resulting gains will be well worth the effort.

Spiritually I, too, am not the same. I have changed, yet it hasn't been easy—on the conscious level. Change has always been difficult from the concrete, hard-fact perspective. But now I feel different: what happens in my life takes on a new meaning. Courses of events do not just occur; they are meant to occur, although I believe that everyone has free will to interpret and act upon situations in whatever manner he or she may choose.

Why then do we behave as we do? For me, it's now my belief that our actions are driven by a need to resolve issues in this lifetime that we never resolved in our past-life existences. I know this statement still may have more skeptics than believers. But I hope that those who now read this book will also begin to question—for that's the beginning.

To doubters I like to tell them of the man who attended his first Super Bowl. He was always a scientific, no-nonsense, only-the-facts type of person. But when he arrived at the stadium and took his seat, he looked around and asked his friend, "What's happening? I've been to regular season football games and never felt like this before. It's like electricity."

Yes, he was feeling the high level of energy from others. No, he couldn't measure it, nor could he touch it. Yet it was there and very palpable. Yes, there is a lot out there which is not definable in scientific terms. We are learning more and becoming more accepting of the viewpoint that we don't necessarily know everything.

Carol's past lives help us to understand and look for other possibilities. Her soul reentered bodies once living in other times, in other existences. The physical body, in whatever shape it may take, is only the house or shelter for the soul.

We search diligently, yet it's right within each of us all the time: the memories of our past. We search for our soul and all that's there. What we may find is not only exhilarating, but also can be quite practical for improving our existence and interaction with others in this lifetime.

To all those who have read these pages, I ask you to allow yourselves to have an open mind and a willingness to explore, and then perhaps the desire to search for your soul within.

Appendix A

Success Stories

C arol, being always the curious writer, often had asked me about my past-life work with others. Was it similar to her own regressions? Different? If so, how? Although I was pleased that she was interested in past-life therapy as a treatment modality and not just as she was experiencing it, I was reluctant to influence her thoughts until we completed our project. I determined not to respond during the course of our regressions. She accepted my decision with regret, but with total understanding.

Although she had often teased me about my dogged determination that once I got hold of something I planned to see it through to the finish—such as this book—she obviously was cut from the same bolt of cloth. We had no sooner completed our last session together than she curled up on the chair and said, "Now tell me about the others. You promised you would."

I couldn't help laughing. Carol certainly had made significant progress in her search for assertiveness. But I was happy to comply. Anyone who loves his or her work is delighted to find another soul who is interested in hearing about it. "Shop talk" is most satisfying.

Many of my patients have granted me written permission to discuss their regressions, provided I altered their names and other identifying details. Carol was familiar with this type of situation as many of those she had interviewed for her health care books had granted the same qualified permission to her.

I considered the hundreds of regressions I had conducted over the recent years and finally decided to share with Carol—as well as with the readers of this book—six different regressions.

Opening the notebook in which I kept my notes, I began. "This one we'll call 'Drinking Diane,' although you realize that Diane is not her real name."

Carol nodded. "Have you worked with addictions in your past-life therapy?"

"Yes, it can be successful even with those with severe addictions. Diane was one such patient. We first met when I admitted her to an addictive disease unit at one of our local hospitals. She presented a disheveled state, having become overwhelmed and unable to cope with her illness." As I spoke, I remembered my first meeting with Diane. She had been an extremely troubled young woman. I continued, "In time, she revealed a long history of addiction to cocaine and other drugs."

"How long had she been on them?" Carol asked.

"She began using drugs in her teen years and had often supported her habit by working as a call girl. Frequently, she would be put up in an apartment with all the trappings by a 'john' until he tired of her. Trips abroad with her escorts were not unusual."

Carol just shook her head, waiting for me to proceed.

"As usually happens, however, her extravagant lifestyle did not continue. Gradually, she went from the top to the bottom. In the process, during one of her binges, she was so drugged that she failed to care for an ear infection and eventually lost total hearing in that ear."

"Poor kid," Carol murmured sympathetically.

"It gets worse," I told her. "Slowly and steadily, the course spiraled downward. Diane lost any remaining self-respect and self-esteem she might have had left. Essentially, a fifteen-year destructive path continued."

"Didn't she ever get any help?" Carol interrupted.

"Many interventions were attempted, including hospitalizations in several of the best treatment facilities throughout the United States. But all met with the same negative results."

"I guess you can't help people until they want to be helped."

I nodded. "That's right. However, this time Diane was cooperative during her detoxification and treatment as an inpatient. She participated in her program, but nothing indicated that this hospitalization would be any different from the previous ones.

"Therefore, upon her discharge, I was quite guarded as to her prognosis, despite her protestations that she was motivated this time to totally abstain from drugs and resume a semblance of a 'normal' life. She did, however, agree to come to my office and institute out-patient therapy."

Carol leaned forward. "So what happened?"

"At our first meeting in my office, I spoke about various treatment modalities, including my work with past lives. She brightened immediately. She spoke of her long interest in this area and expressed a desire to explore this dimension."

"Did you regress her? What happened?" The excitement in Carol's voice was obvious.

"Yes, she was able to go into the hypnotic state. Actually, she was a very good subject. During the initial session, she experienced life as a servant."

"Did she know her name? What about the date?"

I knew these were two areas that had frustrated Carol when she was not able to "see them," as she put it. "Yes, Diane was able to give a great many specific details. She said that her name was Clarice Johnson and that she worked for a baron in England during the 1750s. We quickly found a significant time when she was sixteen years of age. The baron was trying to intoxicate her by encouraging her to drink vast amounts of wine. She didn't succumb to him, however, as she became dizzy and left, falling asleep in her room."

"So she has been drinking a long time," Carol said softly.

"The next significant time," I continued, "took place when Clarice was in her forties, while working in a pub called the Rose and Shield. She was a barmaid and apparently drank continually, having problems with alcohol. She would drink and take various men to her room. Following one of these experiences, the man she was with slit her throat with a knife. Curiously, in Diane's present life, she always stayed away from sharp knives, even to the extent of leaving the kitchen when her husband cooked and used knives."

Carol absentmindedly rubbed her throat as she listened. "In the in-between state," I said, "Diane spoke of Clarice's life as being one of waste, one filled with sadness. The feeling also existed of having to fight to obtain what she might want."

"Did you do other past lives with Diane?"

I nodded. "During our next therapy session, she entered into a past life in which she was a woman in the 1920s, living in New England. Once she was at a jazz club drinking.

Friends wanted her to use morphine, as this was the thing to do in her crowd at the time." I looked down at my notes. "Her death was by a car accident. Although she didn't specifically attribute it to the use of drugs, the question was raised. We soon discovered that outside factors had been allowed to cause her unhappiness. Consequently, it became obvious that Diane needed to find happiness within herself."

"She couldn't get away from drugs in any of her lives?" Carol asked. "What about other regressions?"

"In Diane's next past life, she crossed gender and was a man by the name of John Wheeler. John lived in Wisconsin in the 1870s and was a farmer. Overall, this was a positive lifetime, with the lesson learned of needing to work hard.

"Our review after these sessions revealed a common thread of responsibility. Diane agreed that she needed to take care of herself, be responsible for herself, work hard for her own future, and not be dependent on alcohol or other drugs."

"Did she stick to it?" Carol asked, obviously concerned with Diane's well-being.

"We continued to develop past lives," I said. "Once again, Diane found herself as a man. However, she realized that she was somewhat 'different.' This finding was quite significant in that Diane had been born with a congenital deformity which always made her feel odd. She discovered that the purpose of this life and the lessons learned were those of needing to have tolerance and to accept herself for who she was. By not always having to be as others wanted and not rebelling to get people to accept her, she could succeed with who she was."

"Good for her," Carol called out. Then, "What happened to her?"

I reviewed my notes. "Diane's condition improved as we worked with past-life therapy. She continued to be drug free and took part in the program I outlined for her. It included

an active role with both Alcoholics Anonymous and Nar-
cotics Anonymous. Diane was always punctual for her sessions and her progress continued. Being quite bright, she
expressed a desire to reenter school."

"Did she?" Carol interrupted.

I nodded. "Although she felt somewhat ashamed and
older than the so-called 'regular' students, she did enroll in
college. Much to her surprise, she found herself to be quite
capable and to this date has received all A's except for one B.
Her self-esteem and self-image, once minimal, are now
heightened.

"Diane's goals are multiple and the outlook at this time is
positive. She has resumed family interactions. Her lifetime,
once chaotic and disorganized, is now being rebuilt step by
step. The understanding and experiences encountered in
Diane's past lives have, I feel, immensely contributed to her
recovery."

"That's a great story," Carol said. "It's nice to hear a happy
ending."

"Many of them turned out that way," I told her, looking
for another case history to share. Knowing that Carol had
begun to lose weight through what she had learned in past-
life regression, I turned to another story of someone who
had come to me specifically for work with past-life therapy
in regard to her weight problem.

"This was a thirty-five-year-old woman," I began. "I'll call
her 'Sharon' to protect her identity. She had been married
for almost ten years in an emotionally abusive relationship.
She came with many fears—including episodes of panic,
worries about possible sexual abuse, a phobia involving pictures or newspaper accounts of assassinations, as well as
general unhappiness about her ever-increasing weight.

"Sharon entered trance states readily and experienced
several past lives over the course of treatment. But it was
not until one particularly arduous session that she finally
dealt with the concern of weight."

Carol leaned forward with interest. "What happened?" she asked.

"Within the hypnotic state, Sharon described herself as an attractive woman named Clara, living above a saloon in the western United States. She and Raymond, the owner of the saloon as well as her lover, were out on the sidewalk. He was haranguing her about her 'independence' and complained that she wasn't keeping the other girls in line. Raymond's ultimatum was that she could reenter the building, but only if she would change her behavior."

"Did she?" Carol prompted.

"She finally did go back into the building," I recalled, "but reported feeling very upset, as though Raymond owned her. Her feelings of discontent raged, although she admitted that she wasn't prepared to do anything else in life.

"When I took her to another significant time in Clara's life, she found herself in an upstairs bedroom in the same saloon. She was being lectured by Raymond about how lucky it was for her to be where she was. Since he was providing for her and taking care of her needs, her lover said that she should be grateful and appreciative. He grabbed her, with the intention of making love. Clara sadly disclosed that although she wasn't willing to, she gave in and allowed him to proceed.

"The last significant time in Clara's life occurred in a Colorado farmhouse, at a much later age. She realized that she hadn't enjoyed her early years, but also acknowledged the fact that 'my way of getting through the world was through my body.' She did what she did to survive.

"In the in-between state, after Clara's death, she revealed that a lesson learned was that no matter who you are, you can't let others exploit you. One should look hard and find alternatives, even if you think that none are existent. When I asked her how this lesson would be applicable to Sharon, the answer was as follows . . . " Here I picked up my notes and read the quote exactly. "'If you are very attractive, you have to be more careful. One has to set boundaries as other individuals may not be as disciplined as yourself. You have to control the situation as it arises. You need to make sure that the other person will like you for who you are—not to use one's body to get where you want.' You see, the purpose of Clara's life was that she needed to develop more than her physical attributes. She had to learn not to be used."

"But I don't understand," Carol said slowly. "How does that relate to a weight problem? Clara wasn't heavy. Just the opposite. It sounds as though she had a great figure."

"You're right," I told her. "Without any knowledge of Sharon's history, this past-life experience may not have been too meaningful. But remember, as with all of my patients, I had taken a detailed history at our first meeting. Armed with this information, I was able to help Sharon assimilate what she had learned as Clara in order to help her in this present life.

"As a child and well into her teens, Sharon had excelled in ballet. She was quite good and actually had performed in a local company's rendition of *The Nutcracker*. Like most of those in ballet, she was quite slim. Unfortunately, every time she gained weight, her instructor would harass her and she would panic for fear of being banned from future productions. Even after marriage, her body image remained an issue. Her husband constantly raved to friends about his wife's 'great body.' Others also echoed these comments, so it was understandable that she began to question whether anyone liked her for her total being, rather than just her physical appearance.

"A few years before coming to see me, Sharon was dating two men, both of whom wanted to become involved sexually. The two admitted being aroused by her physical attributes. However, she felt disappointed with their attitudes and never did pursue the physical relationship that they desired.

"It was at this point that Sharon unconsciously decided

to gain weight, thus keeping men away who might crave her because of her body. She wanted others to like her, love her, and respect her . . . 'for the total me, not just for what I look like.'

"Now working with the knowledge gained from her past-life experience, Sharon was able to see that she needed to develop other assets. With other choices and new dimensions, she could become comfortable with herself. When this was achieved, she then could start to lose weight."

"What happened to her?" Carol asked. "Did she lose weight?"

"Subsequently, Sharon enrolled in college," I answered, "along with working full time. Eventually, she entered a Ph.D. program. Careerwise, the future looks positive. Thus Sharon has now begun to lose weight. She no longer will be dependent on her looks, as she was in Clara's lifetime. Choices can and will be made; her dependencies have vanished, having been replaced by a feeling of empowerment."

"No wonder you find this work exciting," Carol remarked. "Do you get faster results . . . do you think you helped Sharon more quickly by using past-life therapy than say a more traditional talk therapy?"

"Yes, as you recall from our initial discussions, one of the benefits of this type of therapy is that, through hypnosis, we can quickly get information from the subconscious and begin to work on those particular issues."

"What about phobias?" Carol asked. "My fear of heights vanished just with the one past-life experience. I had been frightened for years . . . "

"Phobias, such as the one you had," I answered, "often respond rapidly to past-life therapy. Frequently it's after one or two sessions, just like yours did. Bob was such a patient. He originally came to my office seeking to understand why he felt such a link to the Roman era. He confessed that images of gladiators periodically filtered through his mind. 'Do you think past-life therapy could explain this to me?' he asked. I did.

"During the initial evaluation, Bob addressed several issues, one of which was a fear of stairs. He also admitted to a
particularly bothersome problem revolving around an
older brother. Bob had always tried to emulate this sibling's
positive behaviors, but many unresolved conflicts remained. For as many pluses, there were an equal number
of negatives.

"Bob was a good subject, quickly entering the trance
state. His first past life, however, surprised him in that he
was a woman. She lived in Atlanta during the 1800s and was
named Alice. Two children had been conceived in what she
described as a stormy marriage. Publicly, her husband, a
prominent attorney, was well thought of. Behind closed
doors, however, he often beat and raped his wife.

"Two significant episodes in Alice's life were discussed
and both involved abuse. The first of these occurred in their
bedroom. After being rejected sexually, Alice's husband became physically violent. He forcefully pushed her toward
the stairs, intending to throw her down. She resisted. Unfortunately, she indicated that this pattern of behavior had
previously occurred.

"The second episode took place when Alice was twenty-
three. This time she found herself at the bottom of the stairs,
having been tossed down the staircase by her husband. Although factually describing what had transpired, she told
all of these incidents with great emotion.

"When I took Alice to the time right before her death at
age forty, she described lying at the bottom of the stairs,
bleeding from the head.

"In the in-between state, I learned that Bob identified
Alice's husband as his brother in this lifetime. Alice needed
to protect and take better care of herself, as Bob now did.
Alice's husband and Bob's brother shared one specific trait:
they both were cruel as well as brilliant. The entwinement
in the relationship was deep and needed to be resolved.

"The other issue, most graphically portrayed, involved

being thrown down the stairs. I found it most gratifying to learn that the day following this initial session, Bob went to a local mall and proceeded to walk down a flight of stairs that he previously perceived as unapproachable. Just as you had done, Carol, Bob had worked through the etiology of his fear during Alice's lifetime and now, following that past-life experience, healing had taken place and the phobia was resolved."

"That's great," Carol said with enthusiasm. "But what about his fascination with the Roman era? The gladiators?"

"Interestingly," I told her, "during subsequent sessions, Bob indeed did have a past life during the Roman Empire. He found improvement in other areas of conflict and reported that his initial desire for further understanding of himself was achieved to his satisfaction."

"Your patients really traveled the globe in other lives," Carol remarked. "Did they ever speak the language of the country?"

"As a matter-of-fact, some did," I recalled. "Although most people describe their experiences in English, because it's their native tongue, I sometimes get surprises." I looked through my notes. "There was a woman who came to see me after having suffered through a major illness for many years. 'Angelica,' as I'll call her, was somewhat shy and reticent, yet emitted an energy that was radiant. Initially reared in Italy, she later came to the U.S. following her marriage to an American.

"Several issues were identified and our past-life work was quite helpful. However, one regression stood out; not because of the material, but in the manner conveyed during parts of this particular lifetime."

Carol leaned forward with interest. "Go on," she said.

"She said her name was Jean," I answered, "and upon leaving the garden she entered a city with red stone buildings. In the streets were horses and carriages."

"That's not unusual," Carol said.

"Wait. Don't be impatient," I told her. "We did go back to Jean's early years. She spoke of living with her mother in a small French town. When I asked her mother's name, she replied, 'Janet.' But she said it with a French accent. Subsequently, she started to respond to my questions in French."

"Maybe Angelica spoke French," Carol speculated. "Or maybe it really wasn't French and only sounded like it. Do you speak French?"

I shook my head. "No, I neither speak nor understand that language. But Angelica's husband had remained in my office during this specific session. He was fluent in French and nodded as his wife spoke, conveying to me that she was, indeed, speaking correctly. We continued with the session and, after achieving our goals, returned to the present. I quickly asked Angelica to converse with me in French.

"She looked confused. 'But I don't speak French,' she said. 'Why would you ask?'

"Her husband confirmed that prior to our meeting that day he had never heard his wife speak a word of French."

"That's fantastic," Carol said, her eyes sparkling. "It concurs with the story that other psychiatrist told me about a young man speaking in ancient German. It would be hard to fake being fluent in a language you didn't know, wouldn't it?"

I agreed and flipped through my extensive notebook to another case. "I chose this regression as an example of not just a specific issue," I said, "but to illustrate a possible 'lifestyle' adjustment."

Carol nodded and sat back in her chair. I could tell she was enjoying these stories. "Sue, a middle-age, energetic, hard-working woman spoke of several problem areas. She presented them openly, was knowledgeable of past-life therapy, and was desirous of trying this form of treatment herself.

"She easily entered the hypnotic state. Going through a purple door, she saw herself as a man named Edward. His dress, in part, consisted of a cloak covering his large shoulders, suede boots, and a tie. His age was somewhere in the 30s or 40s and the location was England.

"During one significant portion of his life, Edward saw himself on a horse in battle. Blood was everywhere and he was scared. But he was a leader and he carried his banner with the emblem of either an animal or shield. The colors were white and powder blue. Still, he remained frightened and questioned if he wanted to be there as he had also left behind a woman of whom he constantly thought. He felt vulnerable, but as a leader, he had to be where he was. There was no choice: he had to perform his duty and be responsible."

"Poor Edward," Carol murmured. "I know just how he felt."

I nodded and continued. "Suddenly, Sue, as Edward, began crying and said, 'Sometimes he doesn't want to be responsible. He wants the simple life. Too many people depend on him.' Edward then went on to describe the battle in its ferocity. He prayed to God that he would be able to return home and, although others died, he survived.

"We went on to another important time in Edward's life and he found himself in his home. His wife was in bed just after giving birth to a boy. Sue described Edward's feeling as one of total happiness. Later, she told of another battle in which Edward survived the initial fighting but was ambushed on the way home and died."

"Sue's past life as a soldier in England was very revealing," Carol said thoughtfully. "He felt vulnerable, but had no choice but to be a warrior and leave those he loved behind."

"Very good," I said. "You're right. Edward had to perform his duties and responsibilities, even though he did not always want to be responsible. He really desired the simple life without so many depending upon him."

"How did that pertain to Sue in her present life?" Carol asked.

"Sue saw now that she needed to rid herself of some of

the heaviness that she was putting on herself in this lifetime," I answered. "Although at times pretending not to be
so, Sue was essentially a very serious and responsible individual. She realized that it would be okay to let go of some of
her self-imposed burdens and give herself the opportunity
to enjoy life."

"Good for her," Carol cheered. Then she added quickly,
"What's next?"

I laughed, knowing she would have liked nothing more
than grabbing the notebook from my hands and devouring
the details of every past life described within it. "Next we
have Barbara, a quiet woman who experienced a change in
perception and abilities following an understanding gained
through our discussion immediately after a particular past-
life session."

"What was the issue?" Carol asked.

"Her inability to use her artistic abilities. Although she
was very talented, something was preventing her from creating."

"Did she work as a creative person?"

"No," I answered. "During the day she was an accoun-
tant, but she wanted to use her creativity. Something was
blocking her."

"So you tried past-life therapy?"

I nodded. "Upon going through the door in the garden,
Barbara saw herself in torn, black pajama-like clothes. She
was a woman in her twenties, with her head recently
shaven. Her location was a barrack compound, enclosed by
a locked fence. We went to a significant time in her life. She
described herself as a child in an apartment with her parents in an Eastern European country. Political unrest was
apparent and her parents, who were both Communists,
ended up in prison for their political views."

"This is better than television," Carol offered, sitting at
the edge of her chair. "Go on."

"Barbara also had contact with many politicians and artists who supported her art work and thoughts during that period." I looked back at my notes. "She next described being forced into the streets by soldiers where she was laughed at and ridiculed by the people. Her destination was a train station and from there she was sent to a locked camp. The young women were put into one area and ordered to disrobe. They then were marched around uniformed soldiers who eventually sexually forced themselves upon her and the others. This occurred repeatedly until she scratched her attacker."

Carol gasped. "What happened to her?"

"She was severely beaten. Then she was taken to a location where her job was to help others, as she was too weak to perform manual labor. However, she continued to be used sexually by both men and women. To survive, she fantasized what she would do to the hated guards if she could."

"How awful!" Carol murmured.

"During her captivity, a continual conflict existed between Barbara's need to balance passivity and temper. Being passive helped her to survive, but she also needed a certain amount of temper to keep her going. One time, however, she couldn't hold back. A male guard wanted oral sex, which she refused. He then hit her and she bit him in return. She pulled a knife, but he quickly raised his rifle and shot her. She died immediately.

"In the in-between state, she noted sadness at being treated in a manner that was so cruel, questioning how people could relate in such a way, especially as she hadn't done anything wrong. After returning to the garden, then coming out of the hypnotic state, we entered into a lively discussion. I suggested that her artistic ability had been stifled because of what happened in that past life. She had been imprisoned and punished because of her creativity and for being different."

"With that understanding, would she have been able to now express herself?" Carol asked.

I nodded. "Two weeks later, she brought in a painting and pictures she had sketched. Although still holding back some, she was able to state, 'There's creativity in my head again. I have a lot more energy now.'"

"Good for her!" Carol exclaimed, obviously pleased that a fellow artist had once again ignited her talents.

CAROL

I found the above case histories to be fascinating. I think they also helped to give me validation for the work we had done together. I knew firsthand, of course, that many of my past-life experiences had been extremely beneficial. But it was important for me to also hear how others had benefited.

My interest was far more than merely idle curiosity. I wanted to know what kinds of people turned to this type of therapy. Who *were* Dr. Klein's patients? They turned out to be just the average individual from all walks of life—some having higher educational degrees and others with no more than an eighth-grade formal education. They were both young and old, manifesting a vast array of personalities. Yet there remained one constant among his patient base: the willingness to search for answers with an open mind.

While past-life therapy is only one of many therapy modalities used to help people with their problems, I found it to be most enlightening and often successful in that changes in behavior occurred in far less time than more traditional forms of treatment. While it's probably not for everyone, it opens new doors for those who are hurting, often from the weight of baggage carried throughout their lives. It was exciting to walk through those doors in search of truth. It is our choice; each of us has free will.

Appendix B

Brief Overview of Reincarnation

"*E* very soul is immortal—for whatever is in per-
petual motion is immortal...By making the right
use of those things remembered from the former life,
by constantly perfecting himself in the perfect mysteries, a man becomes truly perfect—an initiate into
wisdom more divine."—Plato: *Phaedrus*

Many readers of this book may think, "What an exciting
new therapy!" And it *is* exciting, primarily because of the
rapidity and effectiveness of its healing powers. But while
the introduction of past lives into therapy may be a new
concept, the belief in and experiencing of past lives them-

selves is far from a twentieth-century idea.

From the earliest recorded history of humankind, there have been signs of not only a longing to believe that this life is not all there is, but of an actual acceptance and practice of that belief.

In 1904, a Viking ship discovered in a Norwegian field graphically revealed that culture's belief in a future life. Used as a burial ship for Queen Asa, mother of Harold the Fair-haired, a Viking king who reigned in approximately 900 A.D., the craft contained the well-preserved remains of the queen and her serving woman who was killed to accompany her. Also found were iron lamps, a large comb, scissors, a pail of apples, fifteen slaughtered horses, and four hunting dogs. Her loved ones had obviously prepared her well for her travels ahead.

Almost a thousand years before the birth of Jesus, Buddha preached the concept that we are reborn many times to correct wrongs we may have committed until, at last, we reach a state of perfection and a oneness with God.

Past-life regressions raise little excitement in most Eastern cultures, mainly because both Hinduism and Buddhism—two of the major religions in that part of the world—accept reincarnation as a basic tenet of their philosophy. Past lives are factual for these millions of people; thus, remembering and reexperiencing them is not unique or suspect.

Numerous cultures as dispersed as Australia's Aborigines, various South Pacific island nations, African tribes such as the Igbo of Nigeria, the Tlingit Eskimo of Alaska, and many tribes of the American Indian also believe that a human being, like nature, lives, dies, and is reborn, and that each of us is also our ancestor.

Early Christians also accepted the idea of reincarnation. In the *Confessions* of St. Augustine it is written: "Did I not live in another body, or somewhere else, before entering my mother's womb?" (1:6) Both the Old and New Testaments are filled with references that suggest acceptance of reincarnation and the law of karma. It wasn't until the sixth century that acceptance of reincarnation in Christianity wavered. At that point, according to historians, Emperor Justinian determined that all references to it be stricken from public writings from that time on. Apparently, he and those who followed felt that the citizens would not "toe the line" if they believed they might have a second chance to improve in a later life.

Other groups throughout history, such as the Christian Gnostics of Egypt in the second century A.D. and the Cathars of France believed in reincarnation. Even as late as the twelfth century, the Cathars were tortured and murdered for those beliefs.

In his book, *Through Time into Healing*, Dr. Brian Weiss writes, " . . . aside from their belief in reincarnation, the Cathars, Gnostics, and Kabbalists all had another value in common: that direct personal experience beyond what we see and know with our rational minds or what is taught by a religious structure is a major source of spiritual wisdom . . . Unfortunately, since people may be severely punished for unorthodox beliefs, the groups learned to keep them secret. The repression of past-life teachings has been political, not spiritual."[1] Yet, despite the official banning of the belief in reincarnation, it continued to flourish. " . . . among leading Catholic theologians who advocated the philosophy [of reincarnation] during the Middle Ages were St. Francis of Assisi, founder of the Franciscan Order; the Irish monk, Johannes Scotus Erigena; and the Dominican monk, Thomas Campanella. In more recent times Cardinal Mercier, prelate of Belgian Catholics, stated that the doctrine in no way conflicts with Catholic dogma; and Dean Inge of St. Paul's Cathedral in London declared: 'I find the doctrine [of reincarnation] both credible and attractive.' "[2]

More than one author suggests that the Catholic church may have originally developed its belief in purgatory from the initial stages of the in-between state, where the soul rests, acknowledges what was learned by the most recent life, and determines what lessons must be learned in the coming one. It is also interesting to speculate that perhaps the origins of "The Father, Son, and Holy Ghost" were the father who is reborn and returns as his son to correct mistakes from the past, with the Holy Ghost being the guide or spirit from the in-between state.

One of the major exceptions to the reincarnation silencing is found within the modern-day Jewish Hasidic communities. These people still follow the Kabbalah, the ancient mystical writings pertaining to past lives, which state that we all are reincarnated throughout numerous lifetimes, correcting mistakes of our past until we finally attain the state of perfection desired for all souls. Says Rabbi Philip S. Berg, dean of the Research Centre of Kabbalah International, "Reincarnation is not a question of faith or doctrine, but of logic and reason."[3]

" . . . claims for hypnotic age regression have been made for many years dating back into the 1880s and 1890s . . . Colonel De Rochas claimed in 1911 that he was able to regress his subjects to their infancy, birth, fetal period, and then to their previous lives."[4]

Writing the Afterword for Lawrence LeShan's book, *How to Meditate*, published in 1974, Edgar N. Jackson writes, "Jung in his psychoanalytic studies found that there was a quest among his patients for a spiritual meaning for life. Science now affirms that there is justification for such a quest, and though the scientific method cannot go all the way, it can point directions toward a reasonable framework within which the quest may be made. Years ago Alfred Steinmetz said that the great discoveries of the twentieth century would be in the realm of the spirit. It looks as though science is making a major contribution to this search for spiritual meaning."[5]

One of the best-known modern-day scientists who studies the phenomenon of past lives, University of Virginia's Ian Stevenson, M.D., has collected well over two thousand case histories of children—from diverse countries such as India, Sri Lanka, Thailand, Burma (Myanmar), Turkey, Lebanon, Israel, Tlingit (Alaska), and non-tribal United States—who describe past-life memories. Many of these experiences have been verified by others who knew the former individuals and who had information known only to themselves and the deceased. The fact that the children also knew those details and that some of them also spoke in a foreign language that they had no opportunity to learn in their present life led Stevenson to declare that reincarnation could be the only possible explanation.

Reflection, whether it comes through hypnosis and regression or by meditation, helps us to relive past memories that haunt us and, by reliving them, relieve ourselves of their burdens. As Rabbi Philip S. Berg states it: "To relive is to relieve."

Hugh Lynn Cayce, son of Edgar Cayce, wrote in his book, *Venture Inward: Edgar Cayce's Story and the Mysteries of the Unconscious Mind,* "What conclusions can be reached as to the value of hypnosis as a safe doorway to the unconscious? Men who developed special techniques and whose personalities fitted the part became tribal witch doctors in tribal societies, or Franz Mesmers in more advanced cultures. Alternately, such persons have been worshiped or persecuted, depending upon what authorities' toes they treaded upon. In my opinion, hypnosis is a very excellent doorway into the unconscious. In fact, it is such an excellent one that it should be used with the greatest care. The rapid developments taking place in psychosomatic medicine, as well as in the field of endocrinology, may reveal new powers of the unconscious which so far have been only the subject of speculation. Hypnosis may play a very important part in the new discoveries. Men fear the use of great atomic forces which they now have at their disposal. Perhaps they should be in even greater fear of the tremendous powers of mind which can be awakened. 'The secret of the Lord is with them that fear Him . . . ' (Ps. 25:14)."[6]

In his book, *Memories, Dreams, Reflections,* Carl Jung writes, "We must not forget, that for most people it means a great deal to assume that their lives will have an indefinite continuity beyond their present existence. They live more sensibly, feel better, and are more at peace. One has centuries, one has an inconceivable period of time at one's disposal. What then is the point of this senseless mad rush?"[7]

Indeed, the quantum theory of physics, first introduced by Albert Einstein, describes "time"—as we think of it being measured in years, months, days, hours, minutes, and seconds—as a human-made entity. True time, the quantum physicists claim, is simultaneous—with past, present, and future all occurring concurrently and being able to be tapped into at will.

Cultures based on an acceptance of reincarnation tend to "doctor" their patients in a holistic framework, treating the body and soul as one. Africa's "witch doctor" and the American Indian's "medicine man" are two obvious examples that quickly come to mind. But in societies such as ours in the United States, there has always been more of a tendency to split the two—with one medical specialty treating the body and a psychiatrist or other therapist being brought onto the case if the mind needs work.

Interestingly, as the numbers of believers in past lives increases in the Western world, so have the number of health-care professionals caring for the ill with a holistic attitude. Coincidence? I don't think so.

APPENDIX C

SUGGESTED ADDITIONAL READING

*P*resently there are a myriad of books published almost daily on the subject of past lives and past-life therapy. Therefore, it is impossible to include them all. Nevertheless, we have listed some of the books—both old and new—that we found to be interesting on this subject. We have also included a few titles on relaxation and meditation. It is our hope that you might find some of them to be helpful as well and perhaps even enlightening.

Benson, Herbert, M.D., *The Relaxation Response*, New York: Avon Books, 1976.

Berg, Rabbi Philip S., *Wheels of a Soul*, New York: Research Centre of Kabbalah, 1984.

Binder, Bettye B., *Discovering Your Past Lives,* Culver City, Calif.: Reincarnation Books, 1994.

Cayce, Hugh Lynn, *Venture Inward,* San Francisco: Harper & Row, Publishers, 1964.

Chadwick, Gloria, *Discovering Your Past Lives,* Chicago: Contemporary Books, 1988.

Chopra, Deepak, M.D., *Ageless Body, Timeless Mind,* New York: Random House, 1993.

Cockell, Jenny, *Across Time and Death,* New York: Fireside of Simon & Schuster, 1993.

Cranston, Sylvia, & Williams, Carey, *Reincarnation: A New Horizon in Science, Religion, and Society,* New York: Crown Publishing Group, 1984.

Dyer, Wayne, Ph.D., *You'll See It When You Believe It,* New York: William Morrow & Company, 1989.

Fiore, Dr. Edith, *You Have Been Here Before,* New York: Ballantine Books, 1986.

Gawain, Shakti, *Creative Visualization,* New York: Bantam Books, 1983.

Goldberg, Bruce, *Past Lives, Future Lives,* New York: Ballantine Books, 1988.

Holzer, Hans, *Life Beyond: Compelling Evidence for Past Lives and Existence After Death,* New York: Contemporary Books, 1994.

Langley, Noel, *Edgar Cayce on Reincarnation,* New York: Warner Books, 1967.

MacLaine, Shirley, *It's All in the Playing,* New York: Bantam, 1987.

Montgomery, Ruth, *Here and Hereafter,* New York: Ballantine Books, 1968.

Moody, Raymond A., Jr., M.D., *Coming Back: A Psychiatrist Explores Past-Life Journeys,* New York: Bantam, 1991.

Moody, Raymond A., Jr., M.D., *The Light Beyond,* New York: Bantam, 1989.

Morse, Melvin, M.D., with Paul Perry, *Closer to the Light,* New York: Ivy Books, 1990.

Netherton, Morris, Ph.D., *Past Lives Therapy*, New York: William Morrow, 1978.

Puryear, Herbert B., *The Edgar Cayce Primer*, New York: Bantam Books, 1985.

Siegal, Bernie, M.D., *Love, Medicine, and Miracles*, New York: Harper & Row, 1986.

Steiger, Brad and Francie, *Discover Your Past Lives*, West Chester, Pa: Whitford Press, 1987.

Sutphen, Richard, *Past-Life Therapy in Action*, Malibu: Valley of the Sun, 1983.

Vallieres, Ingrid, *Reincarnation Therapy*, Bath, Avon in Great Britain: Ashgrove Press Limited, 1991.

Wambach, Helen, Ph.D., *Life Before Life*, New York: Bantam Books, 1984.

Wambach, Helen, Ph.D., *Reliving Past Lives*, New York: Harper & Row, 1978.

Weiss, Brian L., M.D., *Many Lives, Many Masters*, New York: Fireside of Simon & Schuster, 1988.

Weiss, Brian L., M.D., *Through Time into Healing*, New York: Simon & Schuster, 1992.

Endnotes

Chapter 2

1. Noel Langley, *Edgar Cayce on Reincarnation*, New York City: Warner Books, Inc., 1967, p. 10.
2. *Ibid.*, p. 44.
3. *Ibid.*, p. 122.
4. *Ibid.*, p. 125.

Chapter 8

1. *Kabbalah for the Layman, Volume III*, by Philip S. Berg, New York: Research Centre of Kabbalah, 1988.

Appendix B

1. Brian L. Weiss, M.D., *Through Time into Healing*, New York: Simon & Schuster, 1992, p. 41.
2. Ruth Montgomery, *Here and Hereafter*, New York: Ballantine Books, 1968, pp. 10-11.
3. Philip S. Berg, *Wheels of a Soul*, New York: Research Centre of Kabbalah, 1984, p. 29.
4. Robert A. Baker, "The Effect of Suggestion on Past-Lives Regression," *American Journal of Clinical Hypnosis*, Vol. 25, No. 1, July 1982.
5. Lawrence LeShan, *How to Meditate*, Boston: Little, Brown and Company, 1974.
6. Hugh Lynn Cayce, *Venture Inward: Edgar Cayce's Story and the Mysteries of the Unconscious Mind*, San Francisco: Harper & Row, Publishers, 1964.
7. Carl Jung, *Memories, Dreams, Reflections*, New York: Random House, 1989.

About the Author

Edward Klein, M.D., has been a psychiatrist in the Tampa area for more than twenty years. A charter faculty member of the University of South Florida's Medical School, he taught in its department of psychiatry as an assistant professor. He is now in private practice.

Dr. Klein received national attention for his work in stress management and past-life therapy. He wrote and produced a video on stress control, which became part of a program developed by the Florida affiliate of the American Heart Association.

Born in Brooklyn, New York, in 1940, he received his medical degree from the University of Louisville Medical School in 1966. His psychiatric residency was at NYU's Bellevue Hospital Center, where he was chief resident. After residency, he entered the military and was a lieutenant commander for two years at a major naval teaching hospital.

For the past twenty years, Dr. Klein has utilized hypnosis in his psychiatric practice and, for the past ten years, has incorporated past-life therapy into treatment plans for many of his patients. A member of the American Medical Association, the American Psychiatric Association, and the American Society of Clinical Hypnosis, Dr. Klein is in great demand as a speaker for both medical and lay groups.

He has been married for twenty-five years to a nurse who is a holistic medicine practitioner. They have two grown daughters.

What Is A.R.E.?

The Association for Research and Enlightenment, Inc. (A.R.E.®), is the international headquarters for the work of Edgar Cayce (1877-1945), who is considered the best-documented psychic of the twentieth century. Founded in 1931, the A.R.E. consists of a community of people from all walks of life and spiritual traditions, who have found meaningful and life-transformative insights from the readings of Edgar Cayce.

Although A.R.E. headquarters is located in Virginia Beach, Virginia—where visitors are always welcome—the A.R.E. community is a global network of individuals who offer conferences, educational activities, and fellowship around the world. People of every age are invited to participate in programs that focus on such topics as holistic health, dreams, reincarnation, ESP, the power of the mind, meditation, and personal spirituality.

In addition to study groups and various activities, the A.R.E. offers membership benefits and services, a bimonthly magazine, a newsletter, extracts from the Cayce readings, conferences, international tours, a massage school curriculum, an impressive volunteer network, a retreat-type camp for children and adults, and A.R.E. contacts around the world. A.R.E. also maintains an affiliation with Atlantic University, which offers a master's degree program in Transpersonal Studies.

For additional information about A.R.E. activities hosted near you, please contact:

A.R.E.
67th St. and Atlantic Ave.
P.O. Box 595
Virginia Beach, VA 23451-0595
(804) 428-3588

A.R.E. Press

A.R.E. Press is a publisher and distributor of books, audiotapes, and videos that offer guidance for a more fulfilling life. Our products are based on, or are compatible with, the concepts in the psychic readings of Edgar Cayce.

For a free catalog, please write to A.R.E. Press at the address below or call toll free 1-800-723-1112. For any other information, please call 804-428-3588.

A.R.E. Press
Sixty-Eighth & Atlantic Avenue
P.O. Box 656
Virginia Beach, VA 23451-0656